Praise for *The Good Ones*

"*The Good Ones* is a must-read for managers and employees alike. In a world that sometimes has a win-at-all-costs attitude, it is good to read about how you can have long-term success by surrounding yourself with people of high character. From now on I will incorporate character questions when conducting interviews and will look at the ten qualities associated with high-character individuals as part of my hiring process."
— JOHN OWEN, global business director at Thomson Reuters

"I don't know which is more exciting, the tools for recognizing character in the interview process or the 'permission' it gives companies to focus on character in the first place. Either way, this is an important and valuable book for any organization."
— DAVID LEVIN, author of *Don't Just Talk, Be Heard!*
and coauthor (with John G. Miller) of
QBQ! The Question Behind the Question

"Bruce Weinstein has put together a survival kit that just might save your job. Want to get ahead? Read *The Good Ones*, a road map to a better life."
— BOB DOTSON, national correspondent for NBC News and *Today*,
and *New York Times* bestselling author of *American Story:
A Lifetime Search for Ordinary People Doing Extraordinary Things*

"Bruce's ten qualities of high-character employees ring true to me. I've hired hundreds of individuals over the past thirty-five years, and when I've failed in hiring it's almost always been about an individual's character, not their skills. We need more sound character in our workplaces, and this book is a great and entertaining way to learn more about why character matters."
— DAVID L. BROWN, MD, former chair of the Anesthesiology Institute
at the Cleveland Clinic and founder of Curadux

"*The Good Ones* helps individuals and institutions integrate ten character traits critical to success. Dr. Weinstein's expert weaving of valid interview questions throughout each chapter provides hiring managers with tools for identifying good people, but also provides job candidates with legitimate samples of behavior-based interview answers to those questions, which will help them land good positions. Finally, employees can apply this book's recommendations by emulating the ten traits necessary to propel them to the leadership ranks. I will personally keep *The Good Ones* close, regularly referencing its resourceful contents in my daily interactions with clients, colleagues, friends, and family."
— J. KIM SCHOLES, strategic human capital consultant at
Booz Allen Hamilton

THE
GOOD
ONES

Also by Bruce Weinstein

AS AUTHOR

What Should I Do?
4 Simple Steps to Making Better Decisions in Everyday Life

Life Principles: Feeling Good by Doing Good

Is It Still Cheating If I Don't Get Caught?
(for tweens and teens)

Ethical Intelligence: Five Principles for Untangling
Your Toughest Problems at Work and Beyond

AS EDITOR

Ethics in the Hospital Setting

Dental Ethics

Ethical Issues in Pharmacy

THE
GOOD
ONES

TEN CRUCIAL QUALITIES
OF HIGH-CHARACTER
EMPLOYEES

BRUCE WEINSTEIN

New World Library
Novato, California

New World Library
14 Pamaron Way
Novato, California 94949

Text design by Tona Pearce Myers

Library of Congress Cataloging-in-Publication Data
Weinstein, Bruce D.
The good ones : ten crucial qualities of high-character employees / Bruce Weinstein.
    pages   cm
Includes bibliographical references and index.
ISBN 978-1-60868-274-4 (paperback) — ISBN 978-1-60868-275-1 (ebook)
1. Employee selection. 2. Employee motivation. 3. Work ethic. 4. Business ethics. 5. Personnel management. I. Title.
HF5549.5.S38W43 2015
658.3'112—dc23   2014046317

First printing, May 2015
ISBN 978-1-60868-274-4
Printed in the USA on 100% postconsumer-waste recycled paper

 New World Library is proud to be a Gold Certified Environmentally Responsible Publisher. Publisher certification awarded by Green Press Initiative. www.greenpressinitiative.org

10   9   8   7   6   5   4   3   2   1

For Jason Gardner,
an editor who is truly one of the Good Ones

CONTENTS

INTRODUCTION

CHARACTER

The Missing Link to Excellence

Take a look at any job description. What do employers say they're looking for? No matter what the job is, its description focuses on two things: what the employee needs to *know*, and what the employee needs to *do*.

Knowledge and skill are essential qualities in any employee. But are they enough? Isn't there another aspect of a job candidate's profile that is at least as important as knowledge and skill — namely, that person's *character?*

Consider what's at stake. Would you really want to hire an accountant who was at the top of her class in business school if she is also a liar and a thief? What electronics company would want one of the country's leading software engineers on its team if that person lost his temper at every real or perceived slight? If you want to sell your home, would it matter to you that your broker bad-mouths his employer on his Facebook page?

There's a quantifiable cost to businesses when employee behavior is less than exemplary. Employees who are actively disengaged cost U.S. businesses between $450 and $550 billion per year, according to a State of the American Workforce report from Gallup. The typical organization loses 5 percent of revenues each year to fraud, according to the Association of Certified Fraud Examiners' 2014 global survey. The median loss in the survey was $145,000, and 22 percent of the cases involved losses of at least $1 million. Workplace violence costs businesses an estimated $36 billion a year and affects over two million Americans. These statistics suggest a painful truth in business: questionable character is costly.

Why Don't Companies Focus on Character?

Given the importance of character, it's surprising, even disturbing, that companies pay so little attention to it when hiring and promoting people. Why is this the case? I asked many business and thought leaders this question, and here's what four of them had to say.

> "Some companies don't think it's important, or they're not willing to put down a set of behavioral values that they're going to hold people accountable to," observes Joel Manby, president and CEO of Herschend Family Entertainment, the largest family-owned theme-park corporation in the United States, whose holdings include Dollywood and the Harlem Globetrotters.

> "Sometimes companies are reluctant to bring up character in an interview because they're afraid they're not going to get an honest answer or that they'll be inviting platitudes," notes Mary Gentile, director of Giving Voice to Values, a business curriculum piloted in over five

hundred business schools and organizations around the world.

"I can't think of a well-known company that includes references to character in their hiring practices," observes John Spence, whom Trust Across America selected as one of the country's top one hundred thought leaders. John, who is a voracious reader of business literature, notes that "if these books talk about character at all, it is inevitably with respect to the leader of a company, not his or her employees."

Alan Tecktiel, senior HR director at the global law firm Baker & McKenzie, adds that even if companies do acknowledge how important it is to hire people of high character, they tend to do so during the job interview rather than when selecting candidates for interviews.

Given what's at stake, wouldn't it make sense to place character front and center at every phase of hiring and promotion, beginning with the job descriptions themselves? It's time for an in-depth look at what it means to be a person of high character in the workplace and why smart companies hire and promote people like the folks you'll meet in this book:

Brenda Harry, an employee at the Goodwill store in Pearisburg, Virginia, who found $3,100 in cash in a coat she was processing. She turned in the money, even though no one would have ever known if she had decided to keep it for herself.

Janice Piacente, a senior compliance officer who routinely gives her team the credit for implementing groundbreaking ideas that she comes up with.

The twenty thousand employees of Market Basket, a New England grocery store chain who left their jobs after the company's CEO, Arthur T. Demoulas, was fired. Demoulas had fought tirelessly for his workers, and they repaid his loyalty with such a widespread protest that it drew national media attention and resulted in his reinstatement.

These are men and women of high character who have chosen to take the high road when it would have been easy to do otherwise. We'll also hear from high-character people who, by their own admission, made poor decisions at crucial points in their lives, and we'll see how those choices affected them. These include Stanley, an accountant, who says that his reluctance to stand up to a corrupt boss in the 1970s continues to haunt him. He explains how that experience taught him the importance of courage, even when one's job is on the line.

Finally, we'll encounter people for whom the term *high-character* is not fitting. Their stories are told from the perspective of former direct reports, colleagues, and bosses, who suffered the consequences of their dishonorable behavior. They include men and women like these:

Dirk, a bookkeeper at a consulting firm who found himself incapable of balancing the books one quarter and decided to fudge a few numbers. This decision required further lies down the road, until the problem grew so large that he was forced to admit what he'd done. He lost both his job and the trust that everyone had placed in him.

Theodore, a manager whose constant stream of insults, angry outbursts, and refusal to acknowledge the good work of his staff transformed what had been a joyful workplace into a toxic environment. His attitude has prompted at least one senior staff member to look for a new job after fifteen years of excellent work.

Federico, an Italian executive whose pattern of asking for suggestions from his team and then ignoring them completely compromised both his relationships at work and the financial interests of his company.

If you're a manager, you'll see from these stories why smart companies actively recruit and promote high-character employees. Wouldn't you want someone like Brenda Harry to work for you? If you're applying for a job, these stories may spur you to think about how you've dealt with difficult situations honorably. They'll prepare you for questions you may encounter in your interview or prompt you to tell your own stories as a way of demonstrating that you are a person of high character. And if you're seeking a promotion or raise, the stories here illustrate why it's in your best interests to discuss during your performance review the notable choices you've made at work.

Character Is Crucial

This is a book about honorable behavior at work. At the heart of honorable behavior is a simple concept: character. It turns out that character and performance are strongly intertwined. "People who have, for lack of a better term, 'ethical lapses,' are never your high-performing employees," says Kenneth Meyer, vice president of human resources for Community Healthcare Network in New York City. "They're either marginal or poor performers."

So why are there so few references to character in job descriptions? What's behind the reluctance to bring up character in a job interview? "People are afraid that this could be invasive," says Ana Cristina Reymundo, founder and first editor of American

Airlines' *Nexos* magazine. "We don't know how to gauge character. We haven't been trained to gauge character. Perhaps we think that a person's bio or résumé reveals their character, but that's not true."

Another reason that character is overlooked is because it's taken for granted. "There's an assumption that you're already trying to hire someone of high character," notes Kirk LaPointe, executive director of the Organization of News Ombudsmen. "But we don't really test our employees in the interview process. We look at their skill sets, and we check references, but we don't get a good firsthand grip on character until they get in the door. It could be because it's more involved and requires a greater dedication to the recruitment process."

As important as knowledge and skill are in successful employees, "they're needed to play, but they're not needed to win," notes Alan Tecktiel. "Yet as critical as character is, employers aren't sure how to define or measure it."

Then there's the comfort factor. "No one would like to be asked in the first round, 'Are you honest?,'" Kirk says, "but around the area of character, and in particular how someone would handle a difficult situation, that gets into intimate territory, and we're still queasy about that. We're treating the employee/employer process almost like a first date, when you're all on good behavior." Although the reluctance to bring up honesty and other facets of a job applicant's character in an interview is understandable, companies cannot afford to overlook it.

In the interviews I conducted for this book, the most common reasons managers gave me as to why their organizations don't emphasize character in hiring and promoting employees are, first, that there doesn't seem to be a universally understood definition of character; and, second, even if we could agree on what it means to be a person of high character, we don't know how to measure those qualities.

These challenges are not insurmountable. Even if there isn't a one-size-fits-all definition of character, and even if evaluating character is more of an art than a science, companies that place a premium on the character of job applicants and current employees are positioned to succeed in ways that their competitors cannot. Let's first try to make sense of the thorny concept of character.

What Is Character?

Character refers to the most important qualities that define a person's identity. It is revealed not by words but by actions. Character stands in contrast to other qualities that describe a person but don't speak to that person's essential nature.

Consider two coworkers, Joe and Mike. Both are 5´7,˝ both are slightly balding, and both like classic rock. Joe has a slightly disheveled appearance, as does Mike. But Joe is self-obsessed, angry, and loves to tell offensive jokes. When you talk with him, the conversation always ends up circling back to Joe. He doesn't seem to know or care what effect he has on other people.

Mike, on the hand, frequently asks you how you are — and carefully listens to your answer. Mike never fails to thank you for things you've done on his behalf, and you've rarely seen him lose his temper. While these two employees may be similar in their physical appearance, style of dress, and taste in music, there are good reasons to believe that Mike is an employee of high character and Joe is not.

Mike and Joe can't do anything about their height, unless 1970s-style platform shoes become fashionable again. They could do something about their appearance, but being mildly unkempt isn't a serious breach of the dress code at work. And liking one kind of music over another is no different from preferring West

Indian Licorice Mocha Delight ice cream over French vanilla. None of these attributes speaks to Mike or Joe's character. But the way the two men treat other people does.

I'm not suggesting that Joe doesn't deserve to work at your organization. He might do his job well, and he may have wonderful qualities he doesn't reveal at work — maybe he's a good husband, a loving father, and active with a local volunteer organization. But because his behavior at work is often insensitive, self-centered, and off-putting, it's difficult to characterize Joe in the same glowing terms you might use to describe Mike.

Mike is a high-character employee. Joe is not. You may not know precisely how they got that way, but you can be sure that three things have contributed to it.

Time, Practice, and Commitment

Character is developed over time, with consistent effort. Character development is similar to weight training. It takes several trips to the gym every week for months to build strength, and if you stop, your body returns to the way it used to be.

When I was writing my doctoral dissertation, I started lifting weights to help deal with the stress of the work. The first time I tried the bench press, I could hardly lift the bar even with no weights on it. Gradually I was able to lift more and more, until finally people started commenting on how strong my upper body looked. Sometime later I stopped weight training, and those bulging pecs returned to their normal, less impressive proportions.

By the same token, it takes constant effort to develop and sustain the traits associated with high character. In his book *10% Happier*, the ABC News journalist Dan Harris talks about how hard he has had to work to develop patience and presence. An on-air meltdown prompted him to reevaluate the way he was living, and he discovered that developing a mindfulness meditation practice helped him to "neutralize the voice in the head," as he puts it, and live more fully in the moment. Being present and resisting the urge to dwell on the past or future is something he works at — hard — every day. Some days go better than others, but overall, he notes, he is much nicer to be around and much less prone to lose his temper.

Is it possible for Joe to develop the high-character traits that Mike already displays? Yes. With the right management and a willingness to acknowledge his shortcomings, Joe may be able to change. But for this to happen, both Joe and his company would have to make an investment in him that one or both might not want to make. Yet if Joe doesn't change and is promoted to a more responsible position, his problems may have profound consequences for the organization and the people it serves.

Smart companies seek to hire and promote high-character people like Mike for five reasons:

- They make coming to work a more agreeable experience for everyone, which is good for employee morale.
- They contribute significantly to the organization's financial health by being highly productive and developing strong relationships with clients.
- They tend to be loyal to their employers. People like Mike stick around.
- They advance the company's mission of enhancing people's lives.
- They reflect well on the company, which is valuable for its own sake and also promotes positive word-of-mouth.

Assuming that Mike and Joe have the same knowledge and skills, Mike is the more desirable employee, because, at least at work, he is a person of greater character. Mike is one of the Good Ones. But how can a business determine whether the person they're considering hiring is more like Mike or more like Joe? Let's take a look.

Evaluating High-Character Employees

Even if we agree on the qualities that comprise high character, the question remains: How can managers determine whether job candidates and current employees possess these qualities? It's especially difficult to assess the character of job candidates, but there are also some surprising obstacles to evaluating the character of current employees.

Scott Erker, senior vice president at Development Dimensions International (DDI), notes that there are four ways companies can gather information for the purposes of hiring and promotion: tests, work simulations, references, and interviews.

Tests

Companies like DDI create intricate tests to help determine whether a job candidate would be a good fit for a particular job. These tests are often web-based and can be taken on a candidate's mobile device. But multiple-choice and true/false questions can't delve deeply into the ten qualities of high character that we explore in this book.

For example, suppose one of the questions on a multiple-choice test is, "One of your company's clients gives you an expensive watch. The policy at work is that employees may accept gifts worth $50 or less. What would you do?" The choices are:

A. Tell the client that you appreciate the gift but aren't allowed to accept it.

B. Keep it.

C. Donate it to charity.

A problem with using multiple-choice tests for evaluating a job candidate's character is that people sometimes lie about what they would do. Just because a candidate says she would tell the client she couldn't accept the gift or would donate it to charity doesn't mean she believes that's what she would do. She might recognize that her employer wouldn't allow her to keep the watch, so she might choose A or C on the test to demonstrate her high character, even if she knows she would do neither of these things. But even an honest response may not reflect how that person would actually behave in such a situation. A test taker might sincerely believe he would refuse the gift, but when this hypothetical scenario becomes real, he might in fact keep it. We don't always do what we say we would do.

There *is* a place for multiple-choice and true/false tests in evaluating character, however. They're useful for beginning a dialogue about honorable behavior and why some choices are better than others. This is how I use them in my speeches and workshops. We'll see in a moment why and how conversation is essential to evaluating a job candidate's character.

Work Simulations

Work simulations involve putting candidates into the actual context in which they would be employed and observing them. These work better for some occupations (say, teaching) than others (cardiac surgery comes to mind). Evaluating character on the job makes sense for employers who use the so-called temporary-to-permanent hiring process. "One bad seed can really have an impact on your culture," says Mona Bijoor, the founder and chief executive of a wholesale company that hires people on a trial basis. Jon Bischke, the CEO of a recruiting software company, notes that a bad hire can kill a company with a small number of employees, like his, which is why he uses the test-drive model of employment.

But it's difficult to see how companies that hire people in the traditional way could evaluate a job applicant's character through work simulations. These organizations — that is, most businesses in the world — have to use other means.

References

References *should* be a helpful way to evaluate character in a job applicant, but often they aren't. Several years ago, a woman whom I'll call Nell applied for a position as my assistant. I was able to contact only one of the three references she provided, and the way this fellow described Nell, I felt I had stumbled onto someone with the charisma of Oprah Winfrey, the integrity of Mother Teresa, and the graciousness of several First Ladies. When I asked the gentleman how he knew Nell, he evaded the question for a while but eventually revealed that he was her fiancé. Small wonder, then, that he had nice things to say about her. I hired Nell, and shortly afterward she quit when a more attractive job opportunity came along. The moral of the story is that the references a job applicant provides can be deeply biased and don't necessarily present an accurate view of the candidate.

By default, the only other option for prospective employers is to contact a job candidate's previous employers, whether or not the job applicant has provided the information directly. The problem is that for legal reasons, many employers provide only minimal information about former employees, such as the duration of their employment.

Alan Murray, the editor of *Fortune* magazine and former president of the Pew Research Center, carefully listens to anything former employers have to say about job applicants. "Sometimes they'll convey useful information about a candidate's shortcomings even while soft-pedaling that information," he told me. What Alan finds surprising is how rarely prospective employers contact him about employees who leave his organization. "I've been angst-ridden over what I was going to say when someone called me for a reference, but it's seldom I get the call," he said. "I don't know if it's laziness or a failure to understand the value of reference checks." Alan's experiences may be the fallout from the practice of employers' giving little meaningful information during reference checks, which discourages prospective employers from contacting references at all.

Jeffrey Hayzlett, host of *C-Suite with Jeffrey Hayzlett* on Bloomberg Television, believes strongly in checking references, but only when those references are people he knows. He cites a book that had a big influence on him, his friend Bob Beaudine's *The Power of Who: You Already Know Who You Need to Know.* The *Wall Street Journal* called Bob's company "the top executive recruiting firm in college athletics," so Bob knows a thing or two about how to find good employees. Alan Murray, too, has found that having a personal connection with references is a way to get information about job candidates that has played a decisive role in hiring decisions.

References are particularly useful when evaluating current employees using the 360-degree feedback instrument, in which colleagues, direct reports, and supervisors — that is, people from an employee's immediate circle — review his or her performance. Until this method of employee evaluation came along, a manager gave a raise or promotion to an employee based on the manager's own assessment of the person's performance. But such a narrow focus can result in what I call the Eddie Haskell syndrome. On the classic 1950s family sit-com *Leave It to Beaver*, Eddie Haskell was ultra-polite to Mr. and Mrs. Cleaver, a wiseacre with his buddy Wally, and a mild bully toward Wally's younger brother, the Beaver. If you judged Eddie only by the way he talked to parents, you'd think he was the most refined kid you'd ever met. But his good manners disguised the fact that Eddie could also act like a real jerk.

As Eddie Haskell's conduct shows, you don't get the whole picture by looking only at how someone treats those who have more power or influence. It's just as important — perhaps even more critical — to find out how an employee treats those who have the same or less power.

Interviews

One of the best tools for evaluating the character of a job candidate or an employee seeking promotion is a direct, in-person, behaviorally focused interview. Although character is revealed by what we do, not by what we say, a manager who pays close attention to a candidate's responses to questions like, "Tell me about a time when you had to stand up to someone in authority," will get a strong sense of the candidate's character.

Interviews are a two-way street, so we'll consider how the interviewers' biases may prevent them from getting an accurate sense of a job candidate's character. We'll also look at ways that interviewers can overcome these limitations.

Why "the Good Ones"?

In the mid-nineties, a friend of mine used the phrase "one of the good ones" to refer to someone he knew. I hadn't heard that expression before, and it stuck with me. Who wouldn't want to be known as one of the Good Ones? Around the same time, a dental professor I knew told me, "There's nothing worse that you can be called than a bad person."

This book's title has two meanings. First, it refers to employees of high character. (It could apply to anyone of high character, but the focus here is on the workplace.) Second, it refers to the ten qualities that are associated with high-character employees. Those qualities are

1. Honesty
2. Accountability
3. Care
4. Courage
5. Fairness
6. Gratitude
7. Humility
8. Loyalty
9. Patience
10. Presence

Honesty is the most important quality of all, so it heads the list. The remainder are all equally important, so, for ease of reference, I'm presenting those nine in alphabetical order.

These qualities are sometimes referred to as virtues. But if we're going to talk about virtue, we must talk about Aristotle, which means we must first talk about Monty Python.

What's Monty Python Got to Do with It?

When you hear the name *Aristotle*, what's the first thing that comes to mind? A college philosophy class? Tom Morris's book *If Aristotle Ran General Motors?* The second husband of Jacqueline Kennedy Onassis? Or Monty Python's "Philosopher's Song," which suggested that Western civilization's great philosophers loved not wisdom but drinking? And what does a philosopher who has been dead over 2,300 years have to do with character in the modern workplace?

The answer is that *The Good Ones* owes its existence to Aristotle's *Nicomachean Ethics*. There are essentially two approaches to thinking about ethics. The first looks at conduct and is primarily concerned with the question, "What should I do?" The second, which originates with Aristotle, asks not, "What should I *do?*" but rather, "Who should I *be?*"

The conduct-based approach to ethics is about solving quandaries such as these:

A. You're standing in line at Starbucks and overhear two colleagues discussing confidential information about a client. Should you say something to them or mind your own business?

B. Your boss asks you to lie. You fear you'll be fired if you stand up to him. How should you respond?

C. You're attracted to your new direct report and suspect the person is attracted to you, too. Would it be acceptable to act on your feelings and ask this person out on a date?

When business ethics or ethics in everyday life is discussed in our culture, it's almost always along these lines. *Dear Abby,* the *Ethicists* column in the *New York Times,* articles in the *Wall Street Journal, Fortune,* and *Forbes,* and heated debates on cable news networks focus on the right way to act in a specific situation. My own work until now has also been concerned with conduct and has been heavily influenced by a masterwork by Tom L. Beauchamp and James F. Childress called *Principles of Biomedical Ethics.* As the title of that book indicates, a conduct-based approach to ethics is based on ethical principles. Applying these principles to the above situations, for example, suggests the following responses:

A. Your colleagues are violating the rule of confidentiality, which is derived from the "respect others" principle (or what Beauchamp and Childress refer to as the principle of respect for autonomy). Because you are in a position to prevent this violation from continuing, it is better to do something rather than nothing. Unless your company requires you to report your colleagues, this means speaking privately with your colleagues about what you have overheard and encouraging them to be more discreet.

B. If the request is more significant than "Please tell me you love my outfit even if you don't," it would be wrong to compromise your own integrity by going along with your boss. He or she is violating several ethical principles, particularly "be fair." Chances are you won't be fired if you stand your ground. You're more likely to encounter serious consequences if you lie for your boss.

C. If you pursue a relationship with a subordinate, you could wind up being accused of sexual harassment or alienating other employees and jeopardizing your career. Office romances are appropriate only when the two parties don't work in the same department and don't have an imbalance of power between them. According to the "do no harm principle" in this situation, the right choice is to look for love elsewhere.

Ethical principles provide a framework, not a formula, for making the right decisions at work and in one's personal life. They're useful for solving conundrums like the ones above. But the character-based approach to ethics is not simply about solving puzzles here and now: it aims to develop traits that prompt us to live our whole lives honorably.

Character is a much murkier concept than conduct, which may explain why discussions about it are not common in either business or our culture in general. When I began conducting interviews for this book, I started the conversations by asking how the subjects hired employees of good character. More often than not I was met with stony silence. Then: "That's a good question." Or "What do you mean by character?" Or a long sigh. I quickly learned that opening an interview with what seems to be an unanswerable question was not a good strategy.

Aristotle discusses character in terms of virtue, which he defines as a mean between two extremes. The virtue of courage, for example, lies somewhere between cowardice (a deficiency of courage) and foolhardiness (an excess of courage). Virtues aren't one-size-fits-all. For a person with a meek disposition, it might require an extraordinary effort to stand up to an office bully, whereas a bold person would have no trouble doing so. *Courageous* would thus be a fitting term for the former person but not for the latter. Even if virtues cannot be quantified in the same way as other abilities (say, performing risk analysis in accounting, or having strong communication skills in any field), they may still be evaluated.

Outside academic circles, *virtue* has overtones of repressed Victorian sexuality, religious fervor, or something our great-grandparents would have fretted about. To avoid these connotations, I talk about *high-character* employees rather than *virtuous* ones, even though from a philosopher's point of view they're the same thing. And to avoid his unfortunate association with dry academic texts (to say nothing of Monty Python), I won't refer to Aristotle very often either.

Wait — What about Trustworthiness?

In reviewing the ten qualities above, you might wonder, "Why isn't trustworthiness on the list? Isn't that really the most important characteristic of all?" Trustworthiness is essential, and it's hard to imagine having any kind of meaningful relationship with someone you don't trust.

But trustworthiness isn't a single quality. Rather, it comes from a combination of several qualities, particularly honesty, accountability, fairness, and loyalty. If I hire you to work for my organization, The Ethics Guy LLC, it's because I trust you, and the reason I trust you is that you have demonstrated that you tell the truth, you do what you say you're going to do, you treat people fairly, and you won't jump ship in the middle of a project if something better comes along.

You might also wonder why integrity isn't on the list of ten crucial qualities. It's for the same reason. Integrity is not a single trait but rather the expression of many traits. Can an employee be considered to have integrity if he or she is as honest as the day is long but is also a selfish, disloyal, and persistently angry person? No. Employees with integrity aren't merely honest: they're also accountable, fair, and patient.

One additional question about the items on this list requires more than a cursory answer: Don't different cultures understand character differently? The answer may surprise you.

Character and Culture

In an episode of *Mad Men* called "The Chrysanthemum and the Sword," the advertising firm Sterling Cooper Draper Pryce tries to land an account with the Honda Motorcycle Corporation. The Japanese executives present a very different way of doing business than their American counterparts, most notably by avoiding direct communication. They do so not in the way that Japanese culture is often mischaracterized (by saying "yes" when they mean "no," for example), but rather through signals such as not sending a gift the day after their first meeting, which may indicate that the meeting did not go well.

In *Business Insider*, Stuart Freedman observes that "avoiding confrontation, saving face, and keeping harmony are a few of the values that influence how the Japanese communicate disagreement, or for that matter anything they think could be upsetting to another person." Where an American executive might say "no," directly, Japanese businesspeople might "indicate that something might be difficult," or simply remain silent.

These cultural differences do not mean that honesty is an integral component of character for Americans but not for Japanese; rather, they mean that the two cultures both value honesty but express it differently. And that applies to all of the ten qualities we'll examine. "Nobody would argue that patience, for example, isn't important," says Scott Erker. "But the way you demonstrate patience in one culture versus the next *is* different."

Evaluating character has profound implications for the conduct of business today. "Global organizations are struggling with this," Scott notes. "The world is getting smaller, people are competing on a global level, businesses are transferring executives all over the world — picking people from one country and moving them over to another — and they're trying to figure out, 'Who's going to be able to operate where, and how do I know it?' If we were able to come up with a universal character model, that would really help people."

A universal character model is a tall order, one that may be beyond the scope of this humble enterprise, but I will present evidence that high-character employees are reliably distinguished by these ten crucial qualities. I'll also show why it's in a business's own interest to place a much greater importance on looking for people with these qualities than most companies do now.

The Three Groups Who Should Read This Book

Three audiences, with some overlap, will benefit from the stories and discussion in this work:

Managers

You will gain a deeper understanding of ten qualities of high-character employees and why these qualities are so valuable to you and your organization. You'll also learn how to identify them in job candidates and determine whether current employees seeking raises or promotions have demonstrated them consistently. If you're charged with reducing the size of your workforce, taking these qualities into consideration will help you make informed decisions about whom to keep and whom to let go.

Job Candidates

It's in your best interests to understand what smart employers look for in employees. You'll put yourself far ahead of other applicants by explaining why these ten qualities of high-character people are fundamental to who you are as an employee and as a person. During interviews, talk about how these qualities help you deliver strong results. Mention them in your follow-up emails. I guarantee that few, if any, of your fellow candidates will be doing this. You will shine — and for good reason.

Employees

Whether you're seeking a raise or a promotion or simply want to remain in good standing in the organization, demonstrating these qualities regularly will help you and your organization succeed. During your performance reviews, explain how you've done so and describe the positive consequences for clients and the organization. This isn't bragging: it's making your supervisor aware of how you benefit the company in ways that go far beyond your knowledge and technical skills. (Note: Because managers of an organization also work for it, I sometimes use the word *employees* to refer to both managers and members of their teams.)

Earlier I stated that honesty is the most important of the ten crucial qualities associated with high-character employees. Let's now see why this is so and how it is essential to the flourishing of organizations and the people who work for them. You'll read true stories that vividly illustrate how employees who evince these qualities help their organizations — and themselves — succeed.

SUMMARY

An employee's character is as crucial to an organization's success as the employee's knowledge and skills are.

Ten qualities associated with high-character employees are

1. Honesty
2. Accountability
3. Care
4. Courage
5. Fairness
6. Gratitude
7. Humility
8. Loyalty
9. Patience
10. Presence

A NOTE ABOUT
THE STORIES

Every story in this book is based on interviews I conducted or experiences I've had. To protect confidentiality, however, I have sometimes changed identifying characteristics of the people involved, such as their names, where they live, and what they do.

When I was a medical school professor, one of my mentors used to advise, when writing a case study about patient care, "Write it in such a way that the people it's about won't recognize themselves." It's a good rule, and I've followed it here when necessary to honor a subject's wish to be anonymous.

You'll know I've applied this rule when the story you're reading introduces someone only by a first name. That isn't the person's real name. In some stories, subjects allowed me to use their names but asked me to mask the identity of other people, which I've done.

TEN CRUCIAL QUALITIES OF
HIGH-CHARACTER EMPLOYEES

CHAPTER 1

HONESTY

So shines a good deed in a weary world.

—Willy Wonka to Charlie, after the boy makes a difficult but honest choice,
in *Willy Wonka & the Chocolate Factory*
(originally from Shakespeare's *Merchant of Venice*)

After the closure of the furniture factory where she had been working for twenty years, Brenda Harry found a minimum-wage job at the Goodwill Store and Donation Center in Pearisburg, Virginia (population 2,786). Her job was to process clothes and other items that people deposited in collection boxes around town. She made sure that they were in good condition and that the donors hadn't left anything in the clothing. Most of the time the pockets were empty, but one day in January 2014, she discovered four envelopes inside a suit jacket.

Those envelopes contained $3,100 in cash. This was more than she made in two months of full-time work at Goodwill. If she had pocketed it, no one would have known. But Brenda Harry immediately turned the money over to her supervisor.

When Deb Saunders, chief compliance officer for Goodwill of the Valleys, told me this story, I wanted to know why Brenda didn't keep the money for herself. So I called Brenda and asked her. "I was raised to be honest," she told me. It was that simple. "It doesn't matter if you need the money. It's not yours. So you turn it in. My parents told me that if you're honest, you will get your reward at the end of time. If you're not honest, you will pay for it on Judgment Day."

It's hard to know how many people would do what Brenda did, because the sort of people who would keep the money might not report doing so. It doesn't even matter, really. What does matter is that smart employers hire people like Brenda Harry, because they can trust her.

All of the ten qualities we'll examine in this book are hallmarks of high-character employees, but honesty is the most important one. No matter how knowledgeable or skilled a person may be, if he or she is fundamentally dishonest or doesn't value honesty, that person is detrimental and possibly even dangerous.

What isn't immediately obvious is how honest employees *benefit* the organization. In some cases, a business can quantify a benefit; the Goodwill store in Pearisburg had $3,100 added to its monthly revenue when no one claimed the money that Brenda turned in. But there are other ways that honest employees are a boon to a business, as we'll see.

What Is Honesty?

Honesty is above all a feeling, a disposition, an orientation toward the truth. Honest employees cannot tolerate lying, fudging data, misrepresenting themselves or their companies, or other conduct that displays contempt for the truth. Falsehood in all its forms is a poison to an honest person.

Refusing to Fudge Data

Well before she became senior vice president for strategy and business development at Xerox, Cari Dorman worked as an electrical engineer for a company that had been awarded a contract with the U.S. Navy. Her role was to develop a software program that would measure the likelihood that a transmitted electronic message had reached its intended target. Cari's boss — I'll call him Saul — asked her to change some data in her research because the results were not what Saul wanted or hoped they would be. Cari did not want to because of the potential implications and did not make the changes.

"I knew that standing up to Saul might get me fired," Cari told me. "But I asked myself, 'What if my son were in the navy during a war, and he was relying on my software program for knowing whether a message he sent got through or not?'" With lives on the line, Cari was willing to risk her job for the sake of doing honest research. Her passion for the telling truth and her courage to be true to herself makes her one of the Good Ones.

For reasons Cari doesn't know, Saul eventually was asked to take a cut in pay, and he left the company.

Standing Up to a Dishonest Vendor

Honest employees are truthful employees. Ken Meyer, vice president of human resources at Community Health Services in New York City, told me how an employee's passion for the truth potentially saved lives, certainly vanquished a cheater, and changed the way Ken runs employee orientation sessions.

Marvin was the new director of the fire safety department at a large company where Ken used to work. When he was going through the contracts from various vendors, Marvin noticed that the one who supplied the company's many fire extinguishers had never inspected them. Marvin called the vendor, Bill, to find out what was going on.

"You're supposed to inspect them," Bill said.

"Um, no I'm not. That's your job," Marvin replied.

Bill then explained how previous fire safety directors had handled the issue. "All you have to do, Marvin, is go through the building, take a look at the extinguishers, and make a note on where you checked the extinguisher," Bill said. "Then count how many you inspected, let me know how many there are, and I'll send you a check."

"Wait a minute," Marvin said. "You're telling me that after I inspect our fire extinguishers, you'll send a check to me, not to my company?"

"That's right," Bill stated, presumably expecting Marvin to exclaim, "Sign me up!" But that's not how Marvin responded.

Instead he said, "All right, I can't attest to what happened before me, but immediately two things have to happen. Number one, you have to send people to inspect these fire extinguishers. Number two, if you ever suggest anything dishonest like that to me again, I am going to drop you like a bad habit and you'll never get work here again."

Imagine an employee lighting a small candle on a birthday cupcake intended for a coworker. The employee blows out the match and tosses it into a wastepaper basket that's half full. As he leaves his desk to deliver the treat to his coworker, that match, which is still smoldering, rapidly ignites the contents of the trash can.

This is the kind of problem that fire extinguishers are meant to solve, but if Marvin hadn't stood up to the corrupt vendor, and the nearest fire extinguisher wasn't functional, what might have happened? How many lives would have been permanently altered by a building fire, and how much damage would the business have sustained? What would the company's legal liability have been when the reason for the faulty extinguisher was discovered? How would its reputation have been tarnished, and what would it take to win it back? All of these questions would arise simply because a fire extinguisher wasn't properly maintained.

Marvin told Ken why he did what he did. "Ken, you want to live your life never having to worry about the knock on the door. As in the knock from someone about to say, 'Something came to my attention that I need to discuss with you. Can you please step into my office and explain something to me?' For what would be a relatively small amount of money, you find yourself fired, not collecting unemployment because it's misconduct, and trying to find a job after something like that."

"To this day, in employee training I repeat what Marvin said all the time," Ken told me. "Conducting yourself ethically frees up your mind. Not having to worry about the knock on the door gives you peace of mind while you're at work."

The events in this story took place decades ago. Marvin is no longer a fire safety officer. He is an ordained Roman Catholic priest and is the pastor of the parish where he lives.

Being Prudent about Telling the Truth

Doris, a senior manager at an automotive parts company, told me a problem she had had recently with her boss, Melanie. "I've known Melanie for years," Doris told me, "and we have a good relationship. Melanie has always encouraged me to speak my mind to her, and I decided it was time to tell her about something that had been bothering me about her for a while."

"What was that?" I asked.

"Well, Melanie has a tendency to tell stories that go on forever. Or at least they seem to. It's more annoying than anything else. And I'm not the only one who feels that way."

"Uh oh," I said. It wasn't hard to see what was coming.

"Yes, I told her. And I added that other people feel the same way, but nobody had the nerve to tell Melanie."

"What happened?"

"It was as if I'd slapped her on the face. She just stared at me for what seemed like an eternity. Then she told me to leave her office. I felt terrible and couldn't sleep that night. The next day I apologized. I didn't even try to justify what I said. I know it was wrong for me to tell her it wasn't just me who thought she has a tendency to ramble. That wasn't my place. And I honestly thought I was doing her a favor. I mean, I'd want people to tell me if they thought I talk too much."

Melanie accepted Doris's apology. Their friendship cooled a bit after that, but it has since recovered.

"I suppose I could have found a better way to tell her the truth," Doris said. I told Doris about the praise-sandwich technique of giving criticism, in which you begin with something sincere but flattering, after which you mention the behavior that bothers you, and you end with something positive.

"Maybe that would work," Doris told me, "but that could also backfire. Just because Melanie says she wants me to speak my mind with her doesn't mean she wants to hear criticism about herself. I do think she needs to be mindful of our time, but her storytelling style is something I guess we'll just have to put up with."

In the introduction, I mentioned that my concept of character is derived from the work of Aristotle. One of the critical components of character for Aristotle is *phronesis,* a Greek word that is usually translated as "practical wisdom" or "prudence." It's what Kenny Rogers sings about in Don Schlitz's song "The Gambler": knowing when to hold 'em, knowing when to fold 'em, knowing when to walk away, and when to run.

Doris learned the hard way that just because people say they want you to be honest with them doesn't mean they want to hear about their shortcomings. Doris is now more careful with how truthful she is with her boss about Melanie's bothersome traits.

"Besides," Doris added, "I'll bet there are things I do that annoy Melanie that she doesn't tell me about."

Most of the time, honesty is a sign of high character. But, as we'll see throughout this book, high-character employees know when to exhibit a particular quality and when to keep it to themselves.

The Consequences of Dishonesty

Ripping Off Restaurants: Considering a Single Dishonest Act

Jerry Seinfeld once said, "A date is a job interview that lasts all night." I wish I'd kept that observation in mind during a date I had early in a relationship with a woman I'll call Penny.

It was my birthday, and Penny took me out to dinner at an upscale restaurant. We began the evening at the bar, but our table was ready before we'd finished our drinks. The hostess told us she would take our drinks to the table and have the bar tab transferred to the check. We finished our meal, the check arrived, and lo and behold, the drinks weren't listed.

"I guess they're a gift!" Penny said in all seriousness. I told her that didn't seem likely, but because it was early in our relationship, and I didn't want to start an argument, I let it slide. I wasn't comfortable with that decision, because we were stiffing both the restaurant and the bartender, who wouldn't be getting a tip.

Penny's decision to get two drinks for the price of none was a red flag that turned out to be indicative of her character. Quick to anger, she criticized me frequently and often used personal attacks to make her point. She had no tolerance for criticism when she was on the receiving end. She rarely came to my defense when others treated me poorly.

Of course, she had positive qualities too, and I'm far from perfect. My flaws, however, don't include stealing, which is what

Penny's choice in the restaurant amounted to. Since Jerry Seinfeld is right in likening a date to a job interview, employers who ignore red flags such as evidence of dishonesty do so at their peril.

The Convict and the Firing Range:
Enduring Repercussions of Dishonest Acts

"Dad, will you go to the firing range with me?" Chuck Gallagher's son asked him one day. "Why not?" he responded. Chuck's son had recently bought a pistol and was looking forward to spending some time with his dad at target practice. But when father and son got to the gun range, they were shocked by what they encountered.

"Not only can you not touch a gun here," said the clerk to Chuck after asking a few routine questions, "but you also can't pay for your son to be here. In fact, you'll have to leave."

Chuck wasn't expecting such a hostile encounter, but he admits he shouldn't have been surprised. That's because Chuck is a convicted felon, and losing the privilege to enter a firing range is one of the consequences of his conviction.

In 1986, when he was in his mid-twenties, Chuck had a successful career as a CPA, and his thorough knowledge of what was then a new employee-benefits provision of the tax law earned him an invitation to testify before the U.S. House Ways and Means Committee. But when he fell behind in his mortgage payments, he borrowed money from a client's account to make up for the shortfall. One thing led to another, and before long, Chuck was running a Ponzi scheme. When it eventually caught up with him, he was convicted of one count of embezzlement and one count of tax evasion and sentenced to eighteen months in federal prison. He lost his wife, the trust of his business partners, and the good reputation he'd had in Morganton, North Carolina.

Chuck did a lot of soul-searching while in the penitentiary, and on his release, he vowed to turn his life around. He created the Choices Foundation, which supports ethics education for young people and awards scholarships to children whose parents are incarcerated. He now is the chief operating officer of a national company based in South Carolina and has a busy schedule as an ethics speaker. He begins his talks in an orange jumpsuit and handcuffs, which make an impression that's hard to forget.

F. Scott Fitzgerald wrote that "there are no second acts in American lives," but Chuck Gallagher transformed the poor choices he made in the first act of his life into an opportunity to prevent others from doing the same. Incidents like the one Chuck experienced at the firing range drive home how devastating the consequences of dishonesty can be.

"Not being admitted to a firing range didn't mean a lot to me," Chuck said, "but it did illustrate two important points for my son. First, it showed him that today I am willing to be honest, even though the consequences may be less than pleasant. Second, there are unintended consequences to your actions, and you cannot escape those. Both of those were good things for my son to experience so that he can remain conscious about the choices that he might make and what the consequences might be."

One Strike and You're Out

Many years ago I had the privilege of taking a weeklong seminar in leadership at the Gallup Institute in Lincoln, Nebraska. Donald O. Clifton was the institute's president (you're probably familiar with his protégés Tom Rath, author of *Strengthsfinder 2.0*, and Marcus Buckingham, coauthor of *First, Break All the Rules*), and I'll never forget what Don said about how the organization deals with employees who have done something dishonest, like fudging data in a poll: "They're fired. Immediately."

"Even if it's just a single offense?" I asked him.

"That's right. Because people have to trust that our surveys and polls are conducted with integrity. Otherwise our product is meaningless."

I asked Alan Murray, editor of *Fortune* magazine and former president of another esteemed polling organization, the Pew Research Center, if he thought Don's policy was too harsh. He didn't think so. "The Pew Center sees its greatest asset as the trust that people have in the information the center provides. So anything that has the potential to damage that public trust is an existential threat to the center's work. Trustworthiness is the core of the Pew brand, and the same was true at the *Wall Street Journal*," where Alan used to be managing editor.

The advertising legend Walter Landor once said that "a brand is a promise." The logo of one of your favorite companies is more than just a cool graphic. The company is essentially saying to you, "You can continue to buy this service or product with confidence that we stand behind what we sell. And if we fail you in some way, we'll make it right." Dishonesty at any level of the company threatens that implied promise.

"I'm privileged to have worked for several great brands, and when you think about what makes brands powerful, it's all about trust," Alan Murray added. "The public has a certain understanding that what they're getting when they see that brand is something they can count on and rely on to a higher degree than what they might find elsewhere. I see maintaining the public's trust as my highest purpose."

A company's power, influence, and integrity are a direct function of the honesty of its employees.

Obstacles to Honesty

If honesty is so important and confers so many benefits, why don't we see more examples of it? It's because lying can be beneficial in both the short and long term.

Success through Dishonesty

A young man named David had dreams of making it big in the entertainment business, so he did what a lot of enterprising people in his position do: he got a job in the mail room of the William Morris talent agency. On his application he wrote that he had been a production assistant for a popular TV show (true) and had graduated from UCLA (false). When a fellow worker in the mailroom got fired for having lied on his application about where he'd gone to school, David got nervous. The agency apparently was fact-checking what their employees stated about their histories. What could he do to prevent his lie from being discovered?

For the next six months, David was the first one to show up at work, and he went through every piece of mail the business received. When the dreaded letter from the university finally arrived, David steamed it open and replaced it with a phony letter confirming his graduation. No one was the wiser.

David's story tells us that starting off your career by committing a felony (mail fraud) can be the first step to becoming wildly successful. That's because the David of this story is David Geffen, one of the richest men in the country. He launched the careers of Crosby, Stills, Nash and Young; Joni Mitchell; Linda Ronstadt; Donna Summer; and the Eagles. He produced *Cats*, one of the longest-running Broadway musicals in history, and together with Steven Spielberg and Jeffrey Katzenberg, he created the film studio Dreamworks SKG.

When David tells the story of how his career began, he does so with no sense of regret or remorse, and the PBS documentary in which this story appears, *Inventing David Geffen*, uses sprightly music on the soundtrack to accompany the tale. The message is clear: the lie that David told to get his foot in the door and the lengths to which he went to remain employed are commendable, even virtuous.

The end justifies the means, right? If David hadn't lied on his job application, wouldn't we have been deprived of some of the best entertainment of the past fifty years?

I don't buy it. This is a man, after all, who concocted a clever scheme to prevent the truth from coming out and worked hard to pull off the ruse. Someone with that level of dedication would have eventually found a way to succeed in Hollywood and New York without being dishonest.

But David Geffen did lie, he did become successful, and it's all too easy for the takeaway message to be, "I did it. So can you." When even a staid institution like PBS valorizes behavior like David's, such conduct becomes an example for enterprising young people to follow. David's story is but one of many in which dishonorable behavior leads to fame and fortune. They serve as a Rorschach test for character, and savvy employers might even find a way to use them as such.

Lying to Save Money

Last year, I needed some help with a vexing computer problem, so I placed a help-wanted ad on Craigslist. I've generally had good experiences with the people I've hired this way, so I had no reason to think this time would be any different. Of the dozens of responses I got, one stood out. A fellow I'll call Conrad wrote an impressive email overflowing with details about how he could fix the issues I faced and why he was the best candidate for the job. The letter was also unusual for being free of spelling errors and poor grammar. Here's a guy who not only had expertise in IT — he could write well too! I wrote him back and asked what he would charge for his services.

That's when he lost the gig. He responded, "You can pay me $45/hour by check or $35/hour in cash." It took me a moment to see what was going on. (Call me slow on the uptake; maybe you figured it out right away.) I could leave a paper trail for the IRS by paying him one fee, or I could help Conrad avoid paying taxes on his income.

I told Conrad I wouldn't be needing his services, and he was genuinely perplexed. "I thought I'd be doing you a favor," he replied. But aside from the inherent dishonesty of Conrad's proposal itself, it made me ask, if he's willing to cheat the IRS to do a job, what other corners would he cut?

As the title of Cheri Huber's book has it, *How You Do Anything Is How You Do Everything*. Conrad's willingness to lie, even for the putative purpose of helping me, cost him the job.

Lying to Save Trouble

I had just administered an exam to a dental ethics class, and my assistant Jackie collected the blue books that the students had used to write their essays. When it came time for me to grade them, I asked Jackie where the books were. She couldn't find them and was afraid to tell me so.

Eventually she mustered the courage to let me know that the books were nowhere to be found. She and I were scheduled to go out of town with our boss for a weekend-long workshop. "I can't bear the thought of spending the whole weekend with you angry at me," she confessed, "so I hope you'll please forgive me."

What Jackie didn't know is that I had been in her situation several years before when I was in graduate school. Somehow I'd lost an entire class's blue books that I'd been assigned to grade, and after trying to concoct a believable excuse as to what had happened, I figured that since I was studying for a PhD in philosophy, I should tell my adviser the truth. I was petrified that he would be angry with me and that I might lose the fellowship I'd worked so hard to get, which would mean finding another way of paying for my education.

But my professor surprised me by being compassionate. He wasn't pleased with what had happened, but he could see that I'd made an honest, if careless, mistake, and that there was no reason to make me feel any worse than I already did.

I thought about that professor's response when I listened to Jackie sorrowfully asking me to forgive her. "Of course I will," I told her. I'm not sure if I told her that I'd once done the same thing she had, but I appreciated the courage that it took to tell me the truth, because I knew firsthand how difficult it was to do that.

Both Jackie and I could have lied to our supervisors. It would have been easier than telling the truth. It wasn't pleasant to admit what had happened, but it was the honorable choice.

Evaluating Honesty

Finding Honest Job Applicants

My father once bought a life insurance policy from an agent who was a really likeable guy. Warm, friendly, and a good listener, Eric was just the kind of person you wanted on your team. His impeccable credentials, strong references, and a professional demeanor made him an understandable choice to handle such an important part of my father's financial portfolio.

He also turned out to be a crook.

After my dad discovered that Eric had embezzled thousands of dollars, my father sued him, and I went to the trial. I'll never forget what Eric's own attorney said to the jury: "No one will ever trust Eric again." When your own attorney publicly declares you to be untrustworthy, you've got some real integrity problems. Eric was convicted of embezzlement and sentenced to prison. After his release, he operated a limousine company and died a few years ago at the age of sixty-two.

Had you met Eric, I'll bet you too would have believed him to be an honest person you could trust as your insurance agent. He is an excellent, if tragic, example of how difficult it is to evaluate a job candidate's honesty.

But because honesty is an essential characteristic of the Good Ones, the following questions and sample answers may be helpful to interviewers.

Tell me about a time when you had to tell a direct report an unpleasant truth. What were the challenges and how did you get past them? What were the consequences?

Ross, a senior vice president at an international consulting firm, needed to tell Hazel, his direct report, that she wasn't going to get the promotion she was expecting. "It was partially my fault for not having submitted the correct paperwork on time, which I didn't know I was supposed to do," Ross told me. "Mostly, though, it was our company's bureaucracy that got in the way of Hazel's promotion. Hazel would have found out on her own in six weeks, but I decided that the bad news should come from me. I didn't want her waiting for something that wasn't going to happen."

He fretted for days before talking with Hazel. "I was afraid she would quit, which she would have been perfectly justified in doing. She has been with the company for seven years and has always done a good job. Well, she was very angry when I told her she wouldn't be getting a promotion this time around. But I was glad she felt safe expressing her frustration to me, and it gave us an opportunity to have an open and honest discussion about her role at the firm."

Ross pressed his own supervisor to get involved, and eventually Hazel got both a promotion and a raise. "Hazel told me she appreciated that I told her what was going on," Ross explained. "She knows she can trust me to be straight with her and to fight for her, too. That may be one of the reasons she still works here." Ross could have kept the truth to himself, but his decision to be open with Hazel illustrates the point that honest employees feel compelled to be truthful.

If a job candidate has had supervisory experience, chances are that this question will be relevant.

Tell me about a time when you could have lied to a supervisor but chose to tell the truth. What happened?

Being honest with the boss can be challenging for a good reason: Who wants to alienate the person who has a big say in whether you get a raise or a promotion — or who may ask you to leave?

But recall the story of Jackie, who lost the entire class of dental students' blue books but told her boss (me) what she did. Jackie could have made up some excuse to explain the problem, but she chose the honorable path. I still respect her for having done this.

Have you ever cheated, and if so, what did you learn from it?

Several of the HR managers I spoke with in doing research for this book told me, "You'd be surprised how often people will just come out and tell you about the dishonest things they've done." I agree.

From time to time I interview high school students who are applying to the college I attended. A few years ago, I mentioned to Rob, the young man I was interviewing, that I'd written a book called *Is It Still Cheating If I Don't Get Caught?* I told him how dismayed I was by news reports of cheating in prestigious high schools and colleges and asked him point-blank if he had ever misrepresented himself.

"Yes," he said. "My friends and I have done it more than once. School is so competitive now you have to cheat to get good grades."

Rob got an A for being honest with me and a "Do not admit" recommendation from me on the college evaluation form.

There are two downsides to asking a direct question about dishonesty. First, it immediately strikes fear in the candidate's heart, even if the candidate is fundamentally an honest person. I don't like the idea of making a job candidate squirm. The second is that the question seems to present a no-win situation for the candidate. She may reason that if the she admits to having cheated, she won't get the job (as happened to Rob); but if she lies, she'll be worried about being caught in a lie and rejected for that reason. Only candidates who have never cheated have nothing to worry about (except being believed).

But the savvy interviewer will not reject a candidate simply because he has admitted to cheating. What bothered me about Rob wasn't so much his admission of cheating but the fact that he exhibited no remorse for having done so and even attempted to justify it.

The smart employer looks not for perfection but for an explanation of how the consequences of a dishonorable act affected the candidate and others. It is probably also helpful if the dishonorable act in question occurred a long time ago!

Discerning Honesty in Current Employees

"No company would evaluate honesty in a current employee unless it were already a part of its core values," an HR director told me. "If a performance reviewer is thinking about honesty at all, he or she is more likely to conclude, 'I have no evidence that this employee is dishonest, so he or she must be honest by default.'" In other words, we should assume that people are honest unless we have good reason to believe otherwise.

But why shouldn't honesty be an explicitly stated core value of every company? There isn't a business in the world that could survive for long if most of its employees routinely lied, withheld the truth, or engaged in other dishonest acts. (Insert joke about politics here.) Even for organizations that don't formally recognize honesty as a value, however, managers should still be on the lookout for exemplary honest conduct. When an employee like Brenda Harry does something praiseworthy like returning the $3,100 she found at work, that action should become a part of the employee's record, just as a dishonest act would be. It reveals high character and reminds managers of how vital the employee is to the organization.

Too often, we think of ethics in terms of what people shouldn't be doing and how unethical behavior hurts organizations. That's part of the story but not all of it. Companies already prohibit employees from acting dishonestly, but they need to go further and actively promote honesty as a core value. This means letting dishonest employees go and hiring and promoting honest ones. Honesty isn't the best policy. It's the only one.

Managers charged with promoting employees are misguided if they believe that employees ought to be acting honestly to begin with and therefore don't deserve to have such behavior officially noted. Putting the information in an employee's record tells the person, "We applaud what you did. You helped us, and we won't forget about it." Also, management does change, so noting actions like Brenda Harry's can help the employee during a performance review conducted by a future manager.

SUMMARY

Of the ten crucial qualities of high-character employees, honesty is the most important. It doesn't matter how knowledgeable or skilled an employee may be if he or she is dishonest.

Honest employees are deeply passionate about the truth and have the courage to act on their convictions.

Employers who fail to evaluate the honesty of job applicants and current employees do so at their peril.

CHAPTER 2

ACCOUNTABILITY

The price of greatness is responsibility.
—Winston Churchill

Harvey is a senior manager with an electronic stock-trading company. One of his direct reports, Lisa, was having performance issues. She had a habit of texting friends while she was at work, and this sometimes made her slow to return calls, respond to emails, and attend to other duties. But her mistakes didn't have serious financial consequences for the company or its clients. Because she was a personable, well-liked employee who had a positive effect on employee morale, Harvey struggled with how to handle her shortcomings.

Eventually it came time to manage Lisa up or out. Because of his concerns about Lisa's performance, Harvey put her on probation for two months. He explained that if her work did not improve, she would be fired. During the probationary period, Lisa's performance was excellent. Harvey was startled to see how well she did her work when she set her mind to it. After the two-month probationary period, Harvey told Lisa that she was on track for a promotion, as long as she could focus on her work and represent the company well.

A few weeks later, Lisa made a serious technical error that caused several hundred customer calls to be dropped simultaneously. The company spent tens of thousands of dollars compensating these customers for deals that were affected by the error. Lisa had gone back to texting on the job, and her distraction had led to the technical glitch.

Lisa was fired immediately, but Harvey felt personally responsible for the dropped calls, even though no one could have foreseen that Lisa could have caused a problem of such magnitude. "If I had fired her instead of putting her on probation, none of this would have happened," he told a few of his colleagues. The day Harvey fired Lisa, he went to his own boss, Suresh, and submitted his resignation. But Suresh wouldn't accept it. Instead he did something completely unexpected: he promoted Harvey.

"What Harvey did showed a lot of accountability," one of his colleagues told me. "He took responsibility for what one of his direct reports did, even though Harvey had nothing to do with it directly. Although Lisa did have performance issues for a long time, she shaped up during the probationary period, so Harvey had no reason to let her go. In fact, she'd improved quite a bit."

Harvey is one of the Good Ones, because he took responsibility for a mistake that one of his team members caused. His honorable conduct resulted in a promotion that his colleagues felt was well deserved.

What Is Accountability?

Accountable employees do four things consistently:

- They keep their promises.
- They consider the consequences of their actions.

- They take responsibility for their mistakes.
- They make amends for those mistakes.

Let's consider each of these characteristics in greater detail.

Keeping a Promise

"I'm going to do what I say I'm going to do, and if I don't do it, I'll let you know," Karen Jacobsen says with great passion. Karen, who is known as the GPS Girl, is the Australian female voice of Siri on the iPhone and on some GPS car-navigation devices. An associate who didn't care about keeping promises changed the way Karen conducts her business.

Karen makes her living as a professional singer and speaker. She has shared the bill with Neil Sedaka, Norah Jones, and Christopher Cross and has sung the National Anthem at Fenway Park before a sold-out Boston Red Sox game. Mel, a promoter, had impressed Karen with his charisma, high energy, and enthusiasm, so she hired him to handle the logistics of an event where she wanted to perform. When the event wasn't selling as well as Karen and Mel had hoped, Mel told Karen he wanted to cancel the engagement. "I was shocked he would even suggest such a thing, because I come from a world where the philosophy is 'The show must go on,'" Karen says. "For one thing, we'd hired a lot of freelancers who would stand to lose income if the event were canceled."

Karen hadn't signed contracts with all of the freelancers. "At that time, I didn't always formalize these agreements. Just shaking hands had always worked for me." But Mel wasn't concerned about whether he'd made any promises, even implied ones, so he had no compunction about walking away from the assignment — which he did. As a result, Karen had to cancel the event, because she wasn't equipped to manage it on her own. She contacted all of the freelancers, explained what had happened, and apologized profusely. She was upset at letting so many people down.

There are two ways of looking at this story through the lens of character. One interpretation is that Karen and Mel simply had different values. For Karen, booking a musical event had both a financial component and a people-centered component. It was important to make a profit, but it was also important to honor the implied promise of hiring the freelancers she and Mel had contacted. Mel's only concern was financial, so his decision to cancel the gig was simply a pragmatic one.

Viewed another way, however, Mel's narrow focus on finances wasn't merely different from Karen's broader view: it was dishonorable. Dozens of people who had reason to believe they would earn money from the event (many of whom had probably turned down other opportunities in order to commit to this one) lost out.

Looking at the story this way makes more business sense as well as more ethical sense. By walking away from a commitment, Mel damaged several professional relationships. First, he ruined his chances of doing business with Karen again, or getting a good referral from her. Second, he hurt his chances of working with the freelancers he had approached. Third, the venue Mel had booked will not want to do business with him again, for the same reasons.

In some cases, performers and organizers stand to lose so much money from a poorly attended show that continuing with it does not make sense. In this instance, however, the show was imminent, and for Karen, who values keeping her word above all else, cancellation was not an option.

The relationship between a promoter and an artist is a partnership. It is counterproductive for the two parties to have opposing values. Karen now works with another promoter, Tom, whom she has known for years, who shares her values — and to whom she is married. Tom knows he may have to be willing to take a financial hit on occasion so that performers can count on him to keep his promise. In the years Karen has been working with Tom, however, she hasn't had to compromise her financial well-being to maintain her ethical standards.

"I do still use handshakes from time to time," Karen texted me recently. "However, I now use contracts and require full payment before live engagements. That has been a massive shift in the way I do business, and it's very positive. The experience with Mel definitely was a turning point."

Considering Consequences

Diana Mekota, a recent college graduate, moved back to Cleveland, her hometown, and thought that reaching out to Kelly Blazek, the self-described "Job Bank Mother," would be a smart move. Since Diana didn't know Kelly personally, she did what millions of people around the world do every day to connect with people they don't know: she contacted her through the business networking website LinkedIn.

Most LinkedIn users who get a connection request from someone they don't know do one of two things: ignore it or accept it. A few ask for clarification. Kelly chose to respond in another way. She wrote to Diana and said, "Your invite to connect is inappropriate, beneficial only to you, and tacky. Wow, I cannot wait to let every 25-year-old jobseeker mine my top-tier marketing connections to help them land a job. Love the sense of entitlement in your generation. And therefore I enjoy denying your invite." Kelly added that Diana was "a total stranger who has nothing to offer me," and after several more condescending statements and personal attacks, she ended with "Don't ever write me again."

Perhaps Kelly thought Diana was a casting agent for a remake of *Mommie Dearest*. It's hard to find any other explanation for such a contemptuous message. Ironically, the Cleveland chapter of the International Association of Business Communicators had chosen Kelly as their 2013 Communicator of the Year. In one sense, they were correct to do so: Kelly certainly communicated her contempt clearly and unambiguously. She set out to accomplish a goal — humiliating a job seeker — and succeeded. However, she didn't consider the possible consequences.

Diana posted Kelly's message on other social networking websites, including Reddit, Imgur, and Facebook, and asked readers to "please call this lady out." The message was linked to Buzzfeed and then went viral on Twitter and other social media. The story was picked up by news outlets, including CNN, *Adweek*, and the BBC. Many in the Cleveland business community and beyond pressured Kelly to return her communicator award, which she eventually did. She also apologized to Diana and deleted her own Twitter account, her blog, and everything in her LinkedIn account except her recommendations.

The ethical issues in this story aren't as clear-cut as they might seem. LinkedIn requests from complete strangers can indeed be bothersome, especially if you get a lot of them, as Kelly apparently did. Diana would have shown greater respect for Kelly by asking a mutual friend for an introduction. And Kelly is far from a villain. A Cleveland marketing and sales consultant, Terry Novak, described her as having been "selfless in her efforts to help people in the sales/marketing, PR, and media fields find leads for jobs in Northeast Ohio for a long time." It's also troubling that Diana's revelations made Kelly's private communication a matter of public record, easily and permanently accessible on the internet.

If Kelly's email to Diana were the only stain on an otherwise spotless record of supporting job seekers in Cleveland, one might be tempted to grant Kelly a pass and move on. Who among us hasn't made a colossal error in judgment like Kelly's? But other recipients of hateful communications from Kelly have come forward, indicating that her mistreatment of people is closer to a pattern than to a single, isolated incident.

As Stefanie Moore, an assistant professor at Kent State University's School of Journalism and Mass Communications, told the Cleveland *Plain Dealer*, "This serves as another reminder that we are held accountable for our actions, even more so in our online-driven world. If we're inconsistent in our interactions with our audiences online and offline, we'll be called out. It can take years to build your online reputation and only one slip-up on social media to destroy it. Another lesson: Think before hitting 'send.'"

Professor Moore is right. In a world where work is increasingly conducted online, high-character employees consider the consequences of every text, email, tweet, and online forum post they make at work. Some go further and apply that standard to their online activity outside work.

Back when news was disseminated in physical objects called newspapers, a popular guideline for acting honorably was "Don't do anything you wouldn't want to see as a headline in tomorrow's paper." The story of Kelly Blazek's LinkedIn communications suggests an updated rule: "Avoid writing or saying anything you wouldn't want to go viral."

This sounds like a standard that allows for communicating only trivialities, but it's not as stringent as that. It simply calls on us to consider the consequences of what we write. Freedom has never meant having the right to insult anyone at anytime for any reason. The internet is the most powerful communications tool the world has ever seen, and as Uncle Ben told Peter Parker in the Spider-Man saga, "With great power comes great responsibility."

Some of the Good Ones handle their work-related frustrations by writing an angry response and then deleting it before sending. This tactic offers all of the giddy pleasure of saying exactly what you feel without any of the unpleasant side effects, such as getting fired, jeopardizing your reputation, or being the subject of a social-media campaign. Had Kelly Blazek read David Shipley and Will Schwalbe's book *Send: Why People Email So Badly and How to Do It Better,* she might have thought twice about communicating in this hurtful way.

Taking Responsibility

The head of the marketing department was furious. "I want Brad fired — now!" he yelled to Geri, a human resources director with a large pharmaceutical company. Brad worked in the mailroom, and, during his rounds delivering the mail, he had made a threatening remark to an employee in marketing. Brad's career could have come to an abrupt end that day, but Geri didn't want to move so quickly.

She invited Brad and two witnesses to come to her office to discuss the matter. "Did you really tell someone, 'You better watch your back?'" she asked. Brad denied it several times. After several uncomfortable moments of silence, he asked, "Um, can you please open the window?" Geri could see that he was troubled by the proceedings. "OK, yes, I said it, but I didn't mean anything by it," Brad admitted. " I wasn't actually going to hurt the guy I said it to."

Geri came from a sales background and prided herself on being able to read people well. She believed that Brad was sincere and that letting him go would be a mistake. She told him, "Maybe you didn't mean anything by what you said, but you have to understand that saying 'You better watch your back' can seem threatening to the person on the other end. You can't talk like that if you want to work here."

"You're right," Brad said. "I take full responsibility for what I did." But he went further than that.

Making Amends

Geri told me that Brad had come from a troubled background but that she saw him as "a sweet fellow underneath a gruff exterior." The reason the head of marketing wanted Brad fired, Geri believed, was not so much the remark Brad had made as the way he looked — like a guy who'd had a hardscrabble life. Geri's success in HR is due in no small part to the fact that she refuses to judge a book by its cover.

Brad volunteered to apologize to the person he'd scared and vowed never to repeat the behavior. He pleaded with Geri to be allowed to keep his job. Geri agreed on the condition that Brad take an anger-management course. That couldn't have been an easy thing for Brad to do, but he did it. Now, every time he runs into Geri, he thanks her profusely for helping him become a better employee — and a better person. Recently, Brad was voted Employee of the Month, and he views the incident that set all of this in motion as a turning point in his professional and personal development.

By taking responsibility for his actions, making the necessary amends, and growing from the experience, Brad has demonstrated that he is one of the Good Ones. But so is Geri, who had faith in Brad and knew that it would it be a mistake to let him go. Too many of us take others at face value. Fortunately, people like Geri are willing to fight for employees like Brad who accept responsibility for their mistakes and take steps to move beyond them.

A Strong Work Ethic

"Action-oriented" is the first listing in Ken Sundheim's *Forbes. com* essay "15 Traits of the Ideal Employee." "Stagnant employees won't make your company money; action-oriented employees will," Sundheim writes. The top item in Kevin Daum's article for *Inc.* online, "5 Desirable Traits of Great Employees," is "account-ability." "Employees can be smart, likeable and talented," Daum writes, "but, if you can't trust them to do what they say they'll do, you and everyone else will constantly waste time and energy checking up on their work." Who is right?

They both are. A strong work ethic is a component of account-ability. If there's some confusion about this, it's because we talk about work ethic in psychological or emotional terms. A person with a poor work ethic is called "lazy," while someone with a superior work ethic is a "self-starter" or "highly motivated." This is a mistake. Having a strong work ethic fundamentally means keeping promises to one's employer. That's why it's an issue of character.

Some of us take our work ethic too far, however. Let's con-sider why high-character employees appreciate the difference be-tween working hard and being a workaholic. We'll then address a question that older workers are asking a lot these days: Do Mil-lennials (people born between 1980 and the early 2000s) lack a strong work ethic?

Workaholism and Work Ethic: What's the Difference?

Hubert's life revolves around his job. He sleeps with his smart-phone next to his bed, and it's always on. The first thing he does in the morning is check his email and answer as many messages as he can. It's also the last thing he does at night. In between, Hubert never stops. But Hubert has missed, and continues to miss, important milestones in his personal life. He rarely goes to his children's birthday parties or school band concerts. He fre-quently interrupts dinner with his family to take a call or send a client a document. When he has a cold, he comes to work because he doesn't want people to think he's a slacker. He's overweight, doesn't exercise, and eats a lot of junk food.

Marie works hard, too. She is at her desk promptly at the start of the work day, and she is highly focused at staff meetings, on the phone with clients, and at her computer. She's not a robot: Marie loves to doodle on a notepad when she's at a meeting (a habit that may enhance retention and promote creativity). She watches what she eats, goes to the gym several times a week, and on the rare occasions when she comes down with a cold or the flu, she stays home until she's well enough to be productive at the office. Marie, by her own admission, isn't perfect. Like Hubert, she checks her smartphone for work-related email at home from time to time. But unlike Hubert, she knows this compulsion is neither healthy nor necessary.

Marie has a strong work ethic. Hubert is a workaholic. I know both people, and it's difficult to imagine that Hubert is going to have a long life. He's in his early fifties but looks ten years older. He has developed a chronic illness that, even if it's not caused directly by his workaholism, isn't being made any better by it. One look at Hubert, and you know this man is in trouble. But he doesn't see it that way.

Hubert is defined by his work. His constant preoccupation with his job isn't a sign of a strong work ethic: it's more akin to an obsessive-compulsive disorder. Marie works hard for her clients, but she also makes time for valued relationships outside work. She establishes and maintains healthy boundaries between her work and the rest of her life.

"Kids Today!" Do Millennials Lack a Strong Work Ethic?

A few years ago, I had a Q&A video series on *Bloomberg Businessweek* online called *Ask the Ethics Guy*. Thomas Lanis, director of the Oscar L. Parker Center for the Advancement of Ethical

Standards in Business and Society at East Central University in Ada, Oklahoma, submitted the following question: "Are there generational differences in ethical values? Some of our local employers and some of my business school colleagues seem to think that young people lack the work ethic of their parents and grandparents. What do you think?"

A study conducted at Bentley University showed that 89 percent of the Millennials surveyed said they have a strong work ethic; 74 percent of non-Millennials saw Millennials this way. The latter group was composed primarily of older people — business decisionmakers and corporate recruiters among them — but also included some people younger than Millennials. On the basis of this survey, Professor Lanis's associates aren't the only ones who believe Millennials avoid working hard. But what's striking about the Bentley finding is that almost three-quarters of non-Millennials claimed that Millennials take their work seriously. *That's* the take-away message from this extensive survey.

Do young people really exhibit "luxury, bad manners, contempt for authority, disrespect to elders, and a love for chatter in place of exercise"? This quotation comes from Kenneth John Freeman's 1907 dissertation at Cambridge University. Freeman was summarizing ancient views of young people, and his words are often misattributed to Socrates (a blunder I made myself in my video response to Dr. Lanis's question). Senior members of society have been complaining about the habits of youngsters for eons, but it's time to label those complaints for what they are: prejudice.

Perhaps the people grousing about Millennials are simply jealous, like the old man in Frank Capra's *It's a Wonderful Life* who watches George Bailey (Jimmy Stewart) trying to work up the nerve to kiss Mary Hatch (Donna Reed). Fed up by Bailey's shyness, the gentleman saunters back into his house and mutters, "Oh, youth is wasted on the wrong people!"

The Cost of Failing to Be Accountable

Employees Who Aren't Accountable Don't Stick around for Long

Nadine was an administrative assistant at a large staffing firm. Marcus, her supervisor, told me that she didn't have a lot of clerical experience before he hired her, but she was most enthusiastic about working for the company. "I can teach people *how* to do a job," he said, "but I can't teach them to be passionate about doing it." During the initial phase of her employment, Nadine impressed Marcus by how quickly she acclimated to the work. "Some of her colleagues told me how personable she was, and a few clients said she was friendly and efficient. That counts for a lot."

But the quality of Nadine's work started to suffer. She stopped responding to Marcus's emails and texts promptly. She didn't complete basic assignments she said she was going to do. And she made a lot of excuses for why things weren't getting done. "She went from working to shirking," Marcus said. He gave her many opportunities to improve, but things got worse, not better. Nothing in Nadine's personal life had changed, but for whatever reason, it became clear that Nadine wasn't accountable to her employer. Marcus fired her and quickly found a replacement he can count on.

"Hype artists — people who promise a lot but don't deliver — usually get found out pretty quickly and don't last long," says Jonathan Taplin, whose extensive career in the film, television, music, and financial industries has included producing Martin Scorsese's film *Mean Streets,* working with George Harrison to organize the Concert for Bangladesh, overseeing media mergers and acquisitions at Merrill Lynch, and creating the world's first video-on-demand internet service. Employees who repeatedly fail to do what they say they'll do damage their reputations and their employability, Jonathan adds. Blaming others or making excuses for their mistakes doesn't do them any favors, either.

Or as Melvin Meads, my high school band director, used to say, "We could have the *Tonight Show*'s lead trumpet player in the band, but it wouldn't do us any good if he showed up late for rehearsal all the time." He said this just before telling a latecomer to go home.

Failing to Hold People Accountable Costs Businesses Money

Laura, a senior human resources manager at a large hospital, told me about Hank, an employee who many believed was taking kick-backs from a pharmacy for patient referrals. He had also been a poor performer for a long time. Eventually the company decided to fire him, but since he was a union employee, the company chose to reach a financial settlement with Hank rather than go before a third-party arbitrator, as required by the union.

"We settled for the highest amount I'd ever settled an arbitration for," Laura said. This was partly because there weren't enough people willing to go on the record to document Hank's alleged misconduct, so the company would not have fared well in arbitration. "But part of that settlement," Laura observed, "is the penalty we pay for not having dealt with Hank's substandard work performance. There are financial consequences for failing to hold people accountable."

This is true in nonunion environments too, notes Alan Tecktiel. "When employees are not held accountable until the point when they need to be fired, companies are usually forced to provide a severance package to avoid legal trouble. Depending on the size of the company, this can cost millions of dollars."

Obstacles to Accountability

What gets in the way of being accountable at work?

An Organizational Culture That Doesn't Value Accountability

Wouldn't you expect that after the government bailouts of 2008 and 2009, a company like General Motors would go out of its way to avoid even the perception of wrongdoing? Recently, however, GM has been called before Congress to account for its failure, for over a decade, to recall thousands of defective automobiles that resulted in more than a dozen deaths.

According to CEO Mary Barra, the problem had to do with "bureaucratic processes that avoided accountability." In practical terms, this meant that no one in the chain of command was willing to take responsibility for mistakes. Gretchen Morgenson reported in the *New York Times* that an internal investigation revealed the following common practices:

- Executives learned about defective ignition switches at committee meetings but either took no action or punted the matter to other committees. Because minutes of meetings were rarely taken, it was impossible to discover who had made decisions.

- Some evasive ploys by executives became so common that they acquired names. In the GM nod, attendees at meetings agreed to take action but then adjourned with no intention of actually doing anything. The GM salute entailed a crossing of the arms and pointing outward toward others, indicating that the responsibility belongs to someone else, not me.

- In a rhetorical move worthy of George Orwell's *Nineteen Eighty-Four,* employees were forbidden from using certain words in their written communications. A "problem" became an "issue"; a "defect" was changed to a feature that "does not perform to design."

The buck stops with the CEO, so Mary Barra was on the right track in identifying a systemic resistance to accountability at GM. Now comes the hard part: changing the culture. The jury is still out on whether GM will be able to achieve that.

The Urge to Overpromise

Why don't people follow through on what they say they're going to do? When I fail to keep a promise I make, it's not because I don't intend to keep the promise when I make it. That's what Jean-Paul Sartre calls "bad faith." Rather, it's because I want to please the person who is making the request and don't think about how much effort it will entail.

For example, in 2013 I gave a talk to a group of association executives, and a member of the audience — I'll call her Alison — approached me after the speech and asked me to write an article for her organization's magazine. I was honored and agreed on the spot to do it. As the deadline for the piece approached, I found myself swamped by promises I'd made previously (namely giving talks to other organizations), and I missed the deadline. I contacted Alison, apologized profusely, and asked if I could still write the piece for her.

No dice. The magazine had contracted with someone else. I suspect I'm permanently on the do-not-call list for this group, and I have no one to blame but myself.

Instead of promising Alison right away that I'd write the article, I should have carefully reviewed my schedule to see if I'd have time to take on the project. An honest assessment would have shown me that I would not be able to do it (at least not well).

But I wanted to please her, so my knee-jerk reaction was to say, "Yes, I'd love to do it!" Ironically, my failure to follow through thwarted my desire to please her.

Time, Money, and Energy

Early in my career as a professional speaker, a prestigious high school hired me to deliver a talk on ethics to the faculty. Just as Karen Jacobsen did with Mel, I trusted the person I was working with to honor our agreement. In fact, I had a written contract, which stated that payment was due on the day of the presentation. The school's representative, Enid, assured me the day before the talk that she had the check ready to deliver.

I arrived well before the starting time and asked Enid to confirm that the check would be available after my talk. "Well, I thought I'd have it by now, but I promise I can get it to you tomorrow," she told me. The school was technically in breach of contract, but I didn't see why over one hundred faculty members had to be penalized for a failure they had nothing to do with, so I gave the speech.

The next day Enid told me that she was having trouble getting the check processed. "No later than next week," she assured me. Weeks, then months, passed with no payment forthcoming.

At that point I had the choice of either writing off the loss or taking the school to court. The amount of money at stake wasn't a fortune, but it wasn't insubstantial, either. I felt the client had betrayed my trust, and I also wondered how many other speakers the school might stiff if I didn't fight back. I felt that a lawsuit was justified. So Richard Solomon, an attorney friend of mine, said he would take on my case.

The school didn't bother sending a lawyer to the hearing because they had no defense. It took two years of diligent work on my friend's part, but I received the payment I'd been promised.

My kind lawyer refused to accept payment for his good work, even though it cost him a lot of time and energy to resolve the matter. He agrees with me that it was worth the effort to hold the school accountable for its debt. But it's understandable that many people who suffer losses through someone else's dishonorable behavior choose to move on rather than fight. It can cost a lot of time and effort as well as money to hold promise breakers accountable. Karen Jacobsen told me, "I don't want to have negative energy in my life, which is what going after a deadbeat client would entail."

Employees who routinely fail to be accountable rack up all three costs — time, money, and energy — for their employers. Supervisors have to divert their attention to the errant employees, which also incurs an opportunity cost. A report from the staffing firm Robert Half International reveals that managers spend almost 17 percent of their time at work — or close to a full day out of five — dealing with underperforming employees.

This isn't merely frustrating. It also compromises the company's ability to fulfill its mission and can result in financial losses. Gallup estimates that actively disengaged employees cost U.S. businesses between $450 billion and $550 billion per year. And a 2011 *Wall Street Journal* article by Robert Sutton provides evidence that even a few errant employees can adversely affect a team's or even the entire organization's performance. In spite of what the Osmond Brothers or Aaron Carter may say, one bad apple *can* spoil the whole bunch.

Evaluating Accountability

The following questions may help managers discern a job candidate's level of accountability. The questions also work well during performance reviews of current employees.

Walk me through a typical working day.

Asking a job applicant to provide details of a working day is an attempt to discover what many call the person's work-life balance. The point is to get the applicant's assessment of how work fits in with his or her life. People with a strong work ethic are accountable people, because they keep their promises to their employers to do their jobs well. They're neither lazy nor workaholics.

A predictable response might be, "I'm at my desk every morning by 8:30 and leave no earlier than 5:30." But that doesn't reveal much. Does the interviewee eat lunch at his or her desk while working, or even skip it altogether? Does exercise play a role in the day? What happens before and after work? More work? Time with friends or family?

Recall the different approaches to work that Hubert and Marie have. Hubert works constantly, which compromises his personal relationships and health. Marie works hard when she's at the office and occasionally checks her smartphone when she's home, but she does her best to separate the professional and personal dimensions of her life (no easy feat given our ready access to work and our employers' ready access to us). Hubert is a workaholic. Marie has a strong work ethic yet still has room for valued relationships beyond work.

Evaluating responses to this question requires taking a look at the broad picture the employee paints. Sean, a senior editor I'll talk more about in the chapter on gratitude, is one of the hardest workers I know. He doesn't eat lunch, but he's no workaholic. He has close relationships with family and friends, reads for pleasure regularly, and is an avid theatergoer. But when Sean is at work, he is focused like a laser, and he recently celebrated his twenty-seventh anniversary with the company.

"But this question is too personal to ask, even if it's legal to do so," one might object. Yes, it's personal, but in an entirely appropriate way. The interviewer is trying to get a sense of who the job candidate is. What role does work play in the candidate's life? How much does he or she value having a rich and varied personal life? Asking about the candidate's sex life or religious views is out of bounds; inquiring about work-life balance is not.

And then there's the problem of self-evaluation. How accurate is the job candidate's assessment of his or her work schedule and commitment to getting the job done? It might be close to reality, or it might be a bit off. Answering one question won't provide a full view of who the candidate really is, but it may provide some useful clues.

Describe a situation in which you took responsibility for a mistake you made. What were the consequences to you for doing so?

Brad, the mailroom worker who had threatened a coworker, initially denied what he had done but eventually admitted that he had indeed issued such a threat (even though he said he hadn't intended to follow through with it). Geri, the HR director who believed in Brad, refused to allow him to be fired. Brad accepted the conditions Geri set for staying on and went on to be selected Employee of the Month. In Geri's telling of the story, Brad's background made owning up to his mistake especially challenging. Brad is one of the Good Ones for taking responsibility for his poor judgment at work.

Have you ever taken responsibility for a mistake that a member of your team made? Tell me about it.

As we saw in the case of Harvey and Lisa, a manager who takes responsibility for an error caused on his or her watch is acting honorably.

Of course, it's possible that a job candidate has never taken responsibility for another person's mistake. Perhaps he or she has not had managerial responsibility, is new to the job market, or is simply fortunate that the situation has never come up. Another explanation is that the candidate *could* have taken responsibility but chose not to or never considered doing so. It's probably not useful to probe here, because none of these reasons alone is worth rejecting a candidate for. But an affirmative response can be a sign of high character, and that's why it's worth asking.

SUMMARY

Accountable employees are high-character people because they keep promises, consider consequences, take responsibility seriously, and make amends for their mistakes.

A strong work ethic is a form of accountability, because it involves keeping a promise to one's employer. It is not the same thing as workaholism.

Obstacles to accountability include a culture that doesn't value this quality; overpromising; and the time, money, and energy it can cost to hold people accountable.

CHAPTER 3

CARE

"Who put this thing together? Me, that's who! Who do I trust? Me!" These words, the mark of a true narcissist, are shouted by the character Tony Montana in *Scarface* as the drug empire he has built starts to crumble. Even if you didn't know that Montana was a liar, a thief, and a murderer, it's clear that a statement like this can be uttered only by someone who is frightfully isolated. Speaking of his best friend and wife, he says to himself, "I don't need him. I don't need her. I don't need nobody."

Montana's inability to care about anyone or anything beyond himself makes him a tragic figure, someone whom, paradoxically, moviegoers have been caring about intensely for decades. As I suggested in my book *Ethical Intelligence,* movies like this show us the dangers of caring about no one but ourselves.

In business, the term *care* is generally applied to the business-client relationship. It has given rise to unwieldy terms like *customer care associate* for the people formerly known as sales agents.

But high-character employees care about not only their clients but also every relationship they have in and beyond the workplace. Their secret weapon is that they also care about, and for, themselves.

In this chapter, we'll consider why caring employees aren't merely pleasant to be around but are also good for business. We'll look at how employers who care for their employees benefit in material ways. We'll examine some of the ways in which caring can go awry in the workplace, and we'll conclude with some strategies for evaluating care in job candidates and current employees.

What Is Care?

Care, like honesty, is first and foremost a strong feeling or passion. Where honesty means having a passion for truth, care means having a deep concern for people's well-being and flourishing. Many include animals and the environment among the things they care about. Of course, caring people do more than feel strongly about helping people. They put those feelings into action. Care without action is as meaningless as a G-rated Quentin Tarantino film.

The passion for making a difference in people's lives has a profound implication in the business world. In this context, caring is almost always discussed with reference to *other* people. But if you are a caring person, consider the following syllogism:

Care is the application of your passion for helping people.

You are a person.

Therefore, care means applying your passion *to yourself*
        as well as to others.

A caring employee is, above all else, a servant. I'm using *servant* here not in the way that suggests exploitation, obsequiousness, or a harsh imbalance of power. Rather, it's in the spirit of

Robert K. Greenleaf's pioneering work *Servant Leadership:* "A servant-leader focuses primarily on the growth and well-being of people and the communities to which they belong. While traditional leadership generally involves the accumulation and exercise of power by one at the 'top of the pyramid,' servant leadership is different. The servant-leader shares power, puts the needs of others first and helps people develop and perform as highly as possible."

Caring employees serve their organizations, their clients, and their team members while taking care of themselves, too. The Good Ones see both of these goals as essential to their work.

Caring Employees Are Engaged

Many years ago, a public speaker I know called his client to inform her that his flight had been canceled. The speaker had booked the last flight to the western U.S. on the night before he needed to give his talk. When he bought his airline ticket, he didn't take into account that planes sometimes don't make it out of the airport. He didn't take that fact into account because he didn't care enough about his work.

The client was angry and distraught, much more so than the speaker was. Fortunately for the several hundred people who had signed up for the workshop, she found a member of her group who owned a corporate jet. The pilot flew to the speaker's city on the East Coast, picked up the speaker, and brought him to the client's town at what must have been a substantial cost.

You'd think that after this, the speaker would have bent over backward to make up for the previous night, but he continued displaying an astonishing lack of care. After lunch, he stopped by the hotel casino to play some slot machines. Losing track of time, he arrived at the afternoon session a couple of minutes late. He gave the workshop he had been contracted to do, but neither his heart nor his spirit was fully engaged in the work. Although he got the job done, the way he did it was unprofessional, unethical, and embarrassing.

I was that speaker.

"What business does a guy like that have writing a book about high-character employees?" you ask. It's precisely *because* of my poor choices fifteen years ago that I can speak knowledgeably about how crucial care is in business and what can go wrong when employees don't care. I'm deeply ashamed of having treated that client the way I did, and I decided soon thereafter that I needed to commit to being a speaker or not accept speaking invitations at all. I chose the former and now give myself wholly, and joyfully, to every speaking opportunity I accept. It makes no sense to have a speaking engagement and not be completely engaged in delivering it.

Among other things, I make sure to book flights that allow extra time for delays. When I'm at the event, all of my energy is devoted to giving the client the best possible experience. (When my current clients read this, I hope they'll think the speaker I described earlier is another guy. In a way, he is.)

What Is Engagement?

As my story suggests, a person who doesn't care about his or her work isn't fully engaged in it. *Engagement* is a popular term in business that's in danger of becoming a buzzword and losing a valuable core meaning: engaged employees are those who have an emotional connection to their work and an ethical commitment to taking it seriously. Even something as seemingly trivial as day-dreaming, a form of disengagement, can be potentially serious in jobs where lives are on the line. "Engagement means to stop thinking about your band, or your ex-wife, or your sick dog or anything else and concentrate on doing your job efficiently and safely," says Chris Webb, CEO of Ready for Duty Haul-Off, a construction company based in Burleson, Texas.

The English word *engagement* comes from the French *engager*, meaning "to pledge." In the seventeenth century, it referred to battles or fights; the modern association with marriage began in the eighteenth century. In the business setting, *engagement* speaks to the bond that employees have with the mission of their organizations. Writing for *Forbes.com*, Meghan Biro observes that engaged employees are motivated by "shared values, trust, mission and purpose." As Biro notes, this doesn't mean that such employees don't care about money, status, or power. There's nothing inherently wrong with any of those things. But to be engaged at work means to go beyond the pursuit of one's career and have a solid commitment to helping the organization achieve *its* goals.

Randall Beck and Jim Harter of Gallup, Inc., note that their company's research reveals a distressingly low rate of engagement in the workplace, not just in the United States but around the world. Engaged employees, according to Gallup, are "those who are involved in, enthusiastic about, and committed to their work and contribute to their organization in a positive manner." In 2012, two large-scale studies showed that "only 30% of U.S. employees are engaged at work, and a staggeringly low 13% worldwide are engaged. Worse, over the past 12 years, these low numbers have barely budged, meaning that the vast majority of employees worldwide are failing to develop and contribute at work."

Employees who don't care about their work and are not fully engaged in it aren't merely a nuisance. They're a drain on an organization's two scarcest resources: time and money. Beck and Harter observe that employee engagement is linked to "higher profitability, productivity, and quality (fewer defects); lower turnover; less absenteeism and shrinkage [i.e., theft]; and fewer safety incidents. When a company raises employee engagement levels consistently across every business unit, everything gets better."

"The most important way to have people engaged in their jobs is to make sure that you've done a good job of hiring people in the first place," said Robert Pasin, CWO of Radio Flyer. (CWO stands for "chief wagon officer," an appropriate title for the leader of the family-owned toy company, which Pasin's grandfather founded in 1917.) Pasin knows a lot about hiring engaged people; *Fortune* magazine lists Radio Flyer as one of the twenty-five best small companies in the United States to work for. And according to the CWO, "Over the past ten years, we've grown the company three times."

We continue our exploration of care by looking at how caring employees can embolden everyone in a business, including its owner.

Good-Mouthing: How Caring Employees Inspire Others

One afternoon, when I was with my friend Steve Werner at a restaurant in Denver, I groused about the lousy service we were getting. The details are hazy, but I do remember Steve's response very clearly: "Maybe our server is just having a bad day." This incident occurred years ago, but I've never forgotten it. Until then, most of my complaints to friends would be met with something like, "You think that's bad? Listen to this!" Swapping stories about the minor injustices we'd received was a juvenile game of one-upmanship.

But it's not in Steve's nature to engage in this sort of activity. As a former senior manager with the American Cancer Society and Habitat for Humanity International and now executive director of the International Society for the Prevention of Child Abuse and Neglect, Steve doesn't have the time or inclination to dwell on the negative. He looks at a problem from the other person's point of view to understand what might have caused the kerfuffle to begin with. He talks about the good work people are doing, not about the mistakes they're making. He inspires the people he leads to do as he does. He certainly inspired me.

Steve is one of the Good Ones because he refuses to bad-mouth people. Instead, he good-mouths them. Good-mouthing is the practice of saying nice things about people behind their backs. I'd be willing to bet a portion of my valuable collection of Metallica fan club magazines that in workplaces in the United States and around the world, good-mouthing occurs far less frequently than bad-mouthing does. I'm comfortable making this bet because I Googled "bad-mouthing" and found 1,060,000 results. "Good-mouthing" yielded a mere 37,600. Why? Bad-mouthing may be a vastly more popular concept, but recent research suggests that when people feel good at work, they do better work — and more of it.

In a series of controlled studies, Andrew Oswald, Eugenio Proto, and Daniel Sgroi from the Department of Economics at the University of Warwick showed that people who feel good are up to 12 percent more productive than people who do not. Case studies of AstraZeneca, Ernst & Young, Google, and seventeen other employers revealed significant savings in health insurance costs, greater positive word-of-mouth mention of the employers, lower staff turnover, and higher productivity when employee health and well-being improved.

How does good-mouthing promote employee well-being? Here's a firsthand example. During a morning presentation in 2014 to the Montana Society of Certified Public Accountants, I asked the audience to form pairs and good-mouth someone else in the room. During the exercise, I noticed a considerable rise in the energy level of the room and lots more smiling faces. I then asked for volunteers to share their good-mouthing anecdotes with us.

The people who had been good-mouthed told me later that they had no idea they'd had such an impact on others. A few didn't even remember the nice things they'd done that others were praising them for, and all were glad that they'd learned about them that day. The president of the society reported that at the evening board of directors meeting, members were talking excitedly about the exercise, doing some good-mouthing of their own, and pledging to make this a regular practice.

Caring employees make it a habit of telling others the good things that the boss, coworkers, direct reports, and clients are doing. It's a good thing to do for its own sake, and it makes the good-mouther feel good, too. It's also something we can learn or choose to do. I've known Steve since the early nineties and have rarely heard him say an unkind thing about anyone. I want to be more like Steve and other caring people who take this practice to heart — and to their workplaces.

Caring Employees Do Well for the Business and Themselves

When Eryn Swenson hired a teenager to work part-time at New Creations Beauty Salon in Succasunna, New Jersey, she didn't expect much. Other teens Eryn had employed over the years had spent far more time yakking on their cell phones than doing their jobs. So when Madison came on board, Eryn assumed she'd be like her predecessors: marking time until she went on to other things. Boy, was Eryn mistaken.

"I've never seen anyone work harder than Madison did," she said. "I hired her to sweep the floors of the salon, wash and dry customers' hair, things like that. But she went far above and beyond that. She had much more initiative than some of the full-time employees who had been doing hair for thirty or forty years. For example, she made sure that every customer had a return appointment before they left the premises."

"Wasn't that part of her job description?" I asked.

"Not at all. The beauticians are supposed to do it, but too often they don't. Madison saw that was happening and volunteered to book return appointments with customers. She was so friendly with everyone that the customers immediately took a liking to her and were happy to book new appointments."

It was Madison's friendliness that impressed Eryn. "She had the least glamorous job in the place, but whatever the task at hand was, she did it with a smile on her face. She would sell it, like it was the best, most fun thing she could be doing." In six months, Eryn made her a full-time employee.

There was one downside to Madison's go-getter approach to her job. "Some of the stylists ended up relying on Madison to book return appointments. Their attitude was, 'Why should I do it if someone else will?' This is largely a commission-based business, so it was in a stylist's own financial interest to follow up with clients. But some didn't have Madison's level of initiative, so they deferred to her." (Later in the chapter, we'll return to this story to discuss the downside in more detail and see how companies can manage this problem.)

Some employees were perturbed by Madison's devotion to her work, although Eryn said they tended to be complainers anyway. A few left the salon for other jobs, but Madison's enthusiasm had just the opposite effect on her boss. "Madison motivated me to do better," Eryn observed. "She worked hard to impress me, so how could I let her down?" Because she cared so much for doing right by her employer, and because she consistently brought out the best in just about everyone, Madison is one of the Good Ones.

Caring Employees Promote Your Brand

What can you get these days for five dollars? Not much: a kid-sized popcorn at the movies, a few tracks on iTunes, maybe a couple of cups of java at your local coffee shop.

You can also hire someone through a website called Fiverr .com to stand in line at that coffee shop, start up a conversation with the person in front of them, and tell him or her how great your company's product or service is. This purpose is to create buzz, since positive word-of-mouth advertising is one of the most valuable commodities in business and also one of the hardest to come by. But this is a dishonorable practice, because the promoters don't disclose the fact that they're being paid, and they may not like or even be familiar with what they're extolling. (Not all vendors on Fiverr.com stoop to such tactics.)

There's another way to generate great PR for your company. It requires more work on the front end, but it's honorable and long-lasting. Fred Smith, CEO of FedEx, gives an example of how his company achieves this feat:

> A customer who resides in Canada was visiting the U.S. and purchased two baby walkers for her new grandson. She shipped both to her home in Canada. Unfortunately, the shipment did not have appropriate paperwork, which prevented the package from being imported. The contents had also been damaged during transit. A FedEx employee [whom I'll call Jill] discovered that the damage was significant, the shipment had been destroyed, and replacements were not for sale in Canada. Jill took personal responsibility, located and purchased the two baby walkers locally, prepared the paperwork, arranged for shipment to the customer and monitored the shipment until it was delivered.

Jill had nothing to do with the original paperwork problem. But as a representative of the company as a whole, she still felt a responsibility to the Canadian customer. Here is a superb example of an employee who cared so much about the company's mission that she went above and beyond what her job description called for.

The Canadian customer couldn't believe the lengths to which FedEx went to get the replacements to her. If you were that customer, wouldn't you tell the story to your friends for a long time? What company would you use the next time you needed to send a package somewhere?

Hiring someone through Fiverr.com will get your company a few minutes of publicity, even though your publicist may not have any direct experience with your product or service. Hiring someone like Jill will get your company genuine, well-earned publicity that is much more likely to resonate deeply and last longer with the people you're serving. It also helps if your company empowers its employees to find creative solutions to problems, as FedEx does.

Employees Who Care about Themselves Are Good for Business — and Themselves

I know all too well how difficult it is to maintain a healthy weight. As a public speaker, I'm on the road a lot, and finding healthful food at airports, hotels, and restaurants is a constant challenge. But it's nobody's business but mine if I choose to have a couple of doughnuts for breakfast and a basket of cheese fries for lunch, right? Perhaps. But does that make it right for me to do?

Earlier I referred to several studies that suggested healthier employees are more productive. The Centers for Disease Control and Prevention substantiate that finding and add that such employees "are less likely to call in sick or use vacation time due to illness." Employees with a healthy lifestyle often share those positive habits with members of their family, so they're at less risk of missing work to care for family members who aren't well. Fewer sick days mean that companies have to spend less money on overtime and training replacements to cover for absent employees.

Employees who care about their health serve themselves and their families well, too. Everyone benefits.

This is not a call for employers to discriminate against people who have an unhealthy lifestyle. If a company needs to fill a position and one of the leading candidates is overweight, that fact alone should not disqualify him or her. The point is that caring means looking after oneself as well as others, and people who take care of themselves promote their own interests as well as the interests of their employers. As the next story illustrates, organizations do well to care for their employees too.

Employees Who Are Cared For Are Good for Business

Howard, a producer for a popular satellite radio program, told me how his bosses treated employees who were sick. "I woke up with a fever and sore throat, went to the doctor, and found out I had strep throat. But I was ordered to come to work," Howard said. "I was new to the organization and didn't want to let anyone down, but I was in no condition to work. For one thing, I knew I couldn't be very productive, and for another, I didn't want anyone to get sick by being around me." Howard knew that the smart thing to do would be to stay home, but his boss implied that his job would be at risk if he did that.

Howard dragged himself to work and got worse and worse as the day went on. "I hardly got anything done ," he told me. "And guess what? Several people I worked with, including one of the hosts of the show, came down with strep throat a few days later. Of course, it's impossible to say whether I was the direct cause, but you also can't rule out the strong possibility that I was."

Requiring Howard to report to work when he was sick was just one of many reasons why Howard felt that his employer didn't care about him. "I was just a means to an end for them, a way of getting the show produced. The thing is, when I feel that my employer cares for me, I'm motivated to give them my all."

Howard eventually had enough of being treated with contempt, and he left to work at a small nonprofit organization.

"Gwen, the executive director, cares a lot about me," Howard said. "She would never expect me to do work when I'm incapacitated, and she allows me to have a flexible schedule, since I'm a caretaker for my father, who has dementia. As a result, I work harder than ever for her, and I'm also more satisfied with my career than ever before."

A successful radio station lost a good employee in Howard. "But the reason that organization does so well financially," one might argue, "is *because* of the demands they make on their employees." It's a tempting claim to make, but it turns out to be false. Forcing Howard to come to work with a high fever and strep throat compromised the business, since Howard may very well have passed his illness along to a key member of the team. Less work got done, simply because Howard's bosses demanded that he show up, fever and all. Gwen's nonprofit organization is successful too, and the caring way she treats her employees is a major reason for its success.

Caring employees stay home when they're sick so that they won't infect others and will get better. They care for others as well as themselves. Caring managers don't allow employees to come to work sick, and they send sick employees home to protect others and help the sick ones get better.

Gwen's caring approach to management yielded another positive outcome: Howard has management responsibilities now, and Gwen serves as a role model for how he treats his own direct reports. Both Gwen and Howard are Good Ones.

Caring Managers Acknowledge Good Work

Remember the candy factory scene in *I Love Lucy* where Lucy and Ethel stuff chocolates into their faces after the conveyor belt starts moving too fast for them to keep up? Lucille Ball turned the drudgery of working on an assembly line into one of the most famous comic bits in television history. But a colleague of mine, who worked for years as a manager in a Fortune 100 company and whom I'll call Paul, told me that his corporate job was similar to factory work, and it was no laughing matter.

"I rarely heard when I was doing a good job, but my boss, Bernadette, had no problem letting me know when I made mistakes," Paul said. "Yelling was her big thing. I was just a cog in the machinery, churning out product. As soon as my team would complete one project, it was on to the next, with no acknowledgment of what we'd accomplished. Would it really have required a lot of effort for Bernadette to say, 'Good job, Paul'? The lack of any kind of recognition for my effort got to be demoralizing, and I left. My coworker Layne wasn't so lucky. He ended up in the emergency room from all of the stress of the job."

Is this sort of treatment of employees the only way to achieve excellence? I don't think so, and neither does corporate trainer Jess Todtfeld. Jess is the CEO of Results First Training, which helps executives learn how to give effective presentations and media interviews. Paul's story doesn't surprise Jess. "Bosses like Bernadette think that praising employees amounts to mollycoddling. In their minds, saying things like 'Well done!' is something you get outside of work, not at work," Jess says.

After I presented a talk at the Southeast Mine Safety and Health Conference in Birmingham, Alabama, a miner came up to me and asked me why it's easier to be critical than caring. Perhaps there's a vulnerability in being caring that makes us uncomfortable. When it comes to managing people effectively, however, the smart money is on people like Eryn Swenson, who consistently recognized Madison's good work. Bernadette could learn a lot from Eryn and would be better off as a result.

High-Character Employees Care about Their Public Profiles

Imagine a fellow who is vice president of marketing for a corporate recruiter from Jacksonville, Florida. Let's call him Wyatt and his company A#1 Zenith Headhunters. In the "About" section of his Facebook page, he lists the name of his employer and his position in the company. Now suppose that Wyatt has just posted a selfie in which he has his shirt off and a baseball cap on backward and is surrounded by empty beer bottles. He's holding one bottle of beer and making a silly face for the camera. In a few hours, the photo gets over fifty "likes" and several comments about how funny Wyatt is.

Wyatt does seem like a spirited guy, but posting a photo like this on Facebook and mentioning his role at A#1 Zenith Headhunters does his employer no favors. If your company needs to hire people, wouldn't Wyatt's picture make you think twice about working with A#1 Zenith Headhunters? And even if you aren't bothered by what Wyatt has done, can you assume that other potential clients feel the same way? With so many executive recruiters out there, all it takes is one red flag like this photo to ruin a business opportunity.

But what if Wyatt has made the photo viewable only by friends? What's the harm then? As we saw in chapter 2 with the story of Kelly Blazek, even communications intended for a single person can easily become public. Employees who place a premium on care recognize that as fun as it might be to post a wacky photo like Wyatt's on their Facebook pages, it's not worth the potential damage to their reputations or those of their companies.

Wyatt may do a great job marketing his recruiting firm, and he doubtless has other positive qualities, but given his willingness to jeopardize his own reputation, or his obliviousness to how he might be doing just that, would you consider him to be one of the Good Ones?

Obstacles to Care

Misunderstanding What Care Really Means

Doug is a corporate consultant in the Northeast whom I've known for years. He's kind, considerate, upbeat, and always willing to help. Last month, he was scheduled to give a seminar to a Fortune 100 company in California for more money than he usually makes in a month. But a few days before his flight to the West Coast, he came down with the flu. "What do you think I should do, Bruce?" he emailed me. "I don't want to let this client down."

I had a ready answer, because this is the very dilemma that I use at the beginning of one of my keynote speeches. "Doug, I understand how much this engagement means to you, and it's commendable that you want to keep your promise to the client. But can you really give it your all if you're barely able to speak? I know you can hold the microphone close to your mouth, but you're still not able to be at your best."

"Good point," he wrote.

"Besides," I wrote back, "you're contagious. How grateful will your client be if you give the flu to just one person in the audience? I'll help you find a substitute." Both Doug and I knew several people who could replace him on short notice.

Doug told me he would think about what I said, and I assumed he would take my advice. A week later, we were chatting on Skype, and he told me how the story ended. I was surprised.

"I flew out there and spent the day before the gig resting in my hotel room," Doug said. "I told the client about my condition, and she said I was a trouper to come out there. Still, I know I didn't do the job I'm capable of doing," Doug told me. "What I learned is that I need to have a back-up plan."

I've known Doug for almost fifteen years, and he is one of the Good Ones. He's a loyal friend, a helpful colleague, and one of those rare people who brightens any room he walks into. He cares deeply about doing a great job for every client he has, so it's no wonder his star is rising. But in this situation, Doug expressed his care in the wrong way. His desire to impress a VIP client and claim a handsome fee made it hard for him to see the considerable risks of giving the workshop despite his illness, which included

- passing along his illness to other people while traveling;
- doing a less than stellar job;
- depriving the audience of a great educational experience;
- decreasing his chances of getting a good testimonial from the client;
- sending the wrong message to the audience (namely, that a presenter should always give the talk he or she has contracted to give, no matter how bad he or she feels); and
- winding up in the hospital with pneumonia.

Doug's wish to give the talk is understandable. He is the sole breadwinner in his family of four, and this assignment was a lucrative one. As a speaker myself, I know that a booking with a high-profile client also does wonders for one's self-esteem. Finally, Doug had signed a contract with the client, which, to the Good Ones, is more than a legal document: it's a promise, and therefore a matter of honor and integrity.

Had Doug been able to take a step back and look at his situation dispassionately, however, he'd have seen that the best way to care for his client would have been to find a replacement. The client's needs would still have been met, no one would have been at risk of getting Doug's flu, and whoever Doug found to replace him might return the favor someday.

The good news is that having suffered through this most unpleasant experience, Doug will not make the same mistake again. He has learned better ways for showing his clients, his family, and himself how much he cares. As Will Rogers said, "Good judgment comes from experience, and a lot of that comes from bad judgment."

Intimidated Coworkers

Madison, the young self-starter from the New Jersey hair salon, is a dream of an employee, but when I heard her story, the first thing I thought of was Katharine Hepburn's character from the film *Woman of the Year*. Tess Harding is an award-winning journalist, an expert in political affairs, fluent in several languages, witty, and attractive. The only thing she can't do well is cook (a failing that is presented as a source of amusement in this 1940s comedy). Although Tess is a fictional character and Madison is a real person, both seem almost too good to be true. They certainly present a standard of excellence that very few people can meet.

In fact, some of Madison's coworkers who were decades her senior and made far more money did feel intimidated by her performance and began to slack off. Isn't that an argument against hiring caring people like Madison? Why would a manager want to bring someone on board whose commitment to the company is so great that others are turned off by it?

The alternative to employing go-getters like Madison is hiring only those with a moderate to low level of passion and commitment to the organization. That can't possibly be right. If caring employees like Madison have a deleterious effect on some of their coworkers, the problem isn't with Madison: it's with her coworkers and the managers who keep them on.

Eryn Swenson, Madison's boss, did address the tension in the salon stemming from Madison's enthusiasm. Eryn suggested to Madison privately that she dial down her passion just a little bit and focus on the job at hand. Eryn also complimented the stylists privately and at staff meetings to make sure that they felt appreciated. But Eryn also made it clear that Madison was doing great work and that she would stay.

The employees who felt disinclined to do their jobs well after Madison was hired ended up leaving the business. Those employees were not high performers to begin with, so one can hardly blame Madison for their poor work ethic. Eryn's decision to hire and promote Madison was a service both to the business and to the employees who finally realized that they didn't belong there.

Caring for the Wrong Things

"How much money did we make off this client?" one employee asks another. Imagine you're the client they're talking about. Would you want to continue to do business with them? No one is asking that a business be run like a charity, and *profit* isn't a dirty word. But these two salespeople have a cynical view of their relationship to their clients. Their question implies that maximizing profit is the only thing that matters.

It's also the most common question that Greg Smith, a former investment banker at Goldman Sachs, heard from junior analysts there. But it wasn't just recent college graduates who had such a narrow view of their mission. Smith describes a corporate culture in which greed and contempt for customers was systemic.

By Smith's own account, Goldman Sachs wasn't like that when he started in 2000. "It wasn't just about making money; this alone will not sustain a firm for long," he says. The business "revolved around teamwork, integrity, a spirit of humility, and always doing right by our clients." Smith's clients were worth more than a trillion dollars, but his first concern was doing what he believed was right for them, even if that meant making less money for the company.

Smith claimed that the investment bank's more recent obsession with profit to the exclusion of all else is wrong, but not just because its utter lack of care for customers is shameful. "People who care only about making money will not sustain this firm — or the trust of its clients — for very much longer."

The moral of Greg Smith's tale goes far beyond Wall Street. There are three ways for an employee to care in any line of work. He or she can ask, "How can I advance my own interests within the organization?" Or "What can I do to serve other people?" Or take a third approach and ask, "How can I advance everyone's interests?" Which style of caring is most likely to promote trust, lead to positive word-of-mouth, and bring in new clients while avoiding employee burnout? Which is the most honorable?

All three approaches involve care, but the first is the sort that only Tony Montana would appreciate: it's completely self-absorbed. The second type is completely selfless: only the client's and employer's interests matter. The third type is neither self-obsessed nor self-denying: it is care in the broadest, truest, and most long-lasting sense. That's how the Good Ones care.

Evaluating Care

The following questions and suggestions may be useful in job interviews and performance reviews for evaluating the candidate or employee's commitment to care.

Why do you want this job?

Many years ago, one of the presenters at a leadership workshop I attended discussed how a successful airline decided which applicants to hire as flight attendants. If the person said things like, "I want to see the world," or "It sounds like a lifestyle I'd enjoy," he or she was not accepted. This was a candidate who viewed the job in self-serving terms.

The top-ranked candidates were those who conveyed a passion for serving others. As a passenger, wouldn't you want a flight attendant who genuinely cares about helping you make the best of what can be a stressful, unpleasant experience? Working for an airline brings lots of terrific perks, like free trips and buddy passes, but that's what these benefits are: perks, short for *perquisites*, which Merriam-Webster defines as "a privilege, gain, or profit incidental to regular salary or wages." They're the icing on the cake, not the cake itself.

High-character employees are dedicated to serving others, even if they're not in a service industry. They serve their clients, they serve their bosses, and they serve the mission of their organizations. They're neither selfless nor self-serving. The language that they use to describe what they do indicates a strong commitment to people, so it makes sense for managers to listen carefully when job candidates or current employees explain why they want a certain position.

Tell me about a time when you went above and beyond the call of duty at work.

Jill, the FedEx employee, went to great lengths to replace two baby walkers that had been damaged in transit. This is a testament to her remarkable commitment to serving her clients and, by extension, her company. It is an inspiring story and a superb illustration of what it means to care.

But a winning response to question 2 need not involve such extraordinary efforts. Many years ago I was shopping at a Publix supermarket in Ponte Vedra Beach, Florida. As I was checking out, I mentioned to the cashier that I needed an item but couldn't find it. She walked around from the cash register, headed down one of the aisles with me, pulled the item I needed off the shelf, and handed it to me. This happened probably fifteen years ago, but I've never forgotten it.

The total time elapsed couldn't have been more than a minute, but she truly went above and beyond the call of duty to help me find what I needed, and I still tell people that story. Guess which supermarket I'm going to the next time I'm in Ponte Vedra?

As a manager, how would you deal with employees who come to work with a cold or flu?

When Howard's employer required him to come to work with the flu, he couldn't do his job well, and some of his colleagues — including a national radio host — got sick. Being treated simply as a means to an end prompted Howard to leave his job. His current boss, Gwen, would never think of doing such a thing, and as a result of her caring attitude, Howard has much greater job satisfaction.

How would a high-character person respond to this question? One would hope to hear something like this: "I wouldn't allow someone with the flu to come to work. First, I wouldn't want him or her to make other people at work sick. Second, I'd want the employee to get better, which means staying home and resting. I'd find a way to get the employee's work done."

But what if the employee insisted on coming in? "I'll isolate myself," she might say, "so that I won't get anyone sick. I just don't want to fall behind in my work or give others more to do."

A caring manager would say, "I appreciate your loyalty and dedication, but you can best serve us by staying home and getting better."

That kind of manager is someone I'd want on my team. How about you?

SUMMARY

Caring employees

- have a deep concern for other people and themselves, and they put this concern into action
- view themselves as servants, but not to the exclusion of their own health and well-being
- are careful about what they post in social media
- do better work and are more loyal when their employers care for them, too

CHAPTER 4

COURAGE

It is curious that physical courage should be so common
in the world and moral courage so rare.

—Mark Twain

The space shuttle *Challenger* blew up in the sky on January 24, 1986. People around the world watched with horror as seven astronauts, including a schoolteacher from New Hampshire, lost their lives. In seventy-three seconds, a mission that was supposed to reignite a passion for space exploration turned into a horrific event that no one who watched it live on television will ever forget.

What made this tragedy especially upsetting is that it could have been prevented. In fact, Allan McDonald *did* try to prevent it. McDonald worked for the company that the National Aeronautics and Space Administration (NASA) hired to make the shuttle's solid-engine rocket boosters. But a crucial component of the boosters, the dividers known as "O-rings," had never been tested at ambient temperatures below 53 degrees Fahrenheit. If the O-rings didn't seal the joints of the boosters properly, the boosters would explode and kill everyone on board the shuttle.

On the evening before the launch, the weather forecast in

Cape Canaveral, Florida, called for temperatures in the teens. McDonald was concerned about the O-rings not working properly and warned NASA about the dangers of proceeding, but NASA wanted to move forward anyway. McDonald strongly protested this decision and refused to sign the document that would have allowed the project to proceed. "It's the smartest decision I ever made in my life," he said, but his boss signed for him. The launch proceeded as planned, with fatal consequences.

Courage is usually associated with bravery in battle. That's certainly one example of it, and business leaders sometimes use war as a metaphor to describe what they're up against. *The Art of War* remains a popular book with executives, even though Sun Tzu wrote it with a military audience in mind over two thousand years ago.

But the kind of courage required for physical battle or the struggles faced by C-suite executives and boards of directors won't necessarily help with the problems we encounter regularly at work. Those problems often involve speaking out about injustice and other moral concerns. Allan MacDonald was willing to challenge a complex bureaucracy and risk his career because remaining silent meant allowing innocent people to be put in harm's way. This is the type of courage we'll explore here.

I present four elements of courage in the workplace and explain why businesses need high-character employees like Allan. I'll also provide some questions that managers can use to evaluate courage in prospective and current employees.

What Is Courage?

A ship in harbor is safe, but that is not what ships are built for.
—John A. Shedd

Wherever they work, in large or small companies and in any line of business, courageous employees have the strength of character to say and do things that need to be done. In most cases, this courage has nothing to do with physical strength.

Sherron Watkins hasn't won any marathons, but she put her job and reputation on the line by blowing the whistle on her crooked bosses at Enron. *Time* magazine rightly named her a Person of the Year for standing up to illegal and unethical business practices. She had the moral strength — the courage — to risk her job, reputation, and valued relationships to stand up to the wrongdoing she saw.

Courageous employees are willing to

- tell managers things they need to know, even though they might not want to know them
- fight for their clients and business
- do unpleasant but necessary things
- ask for help

Let's hear from some courageous people who did these things and what the consequences were.

Courageous Employees Speak Up

For thirty years, Alexandra Troy has created gourmet meals for such clients as Volvo, Estée Lauder, Citibank/Citicorp, Brooks Brothers, Lord & Taylor, Macy's, Merrill Lynch, and Tiffany. She is the founder and CEO of Culinary Architect Catering, a private company based in Greenvale, New York. With such a tony client list, Alexandra prides herself on using the best ingredients, hiring the most courteous servers, and creating dining experiences that make the hosts shine.

Fifty people work for Alexandra, and she holds them to the same exacting standards she sets for herself. Since she can't attend every one of her events, she depends on her contractors to do right by Culinary Architect. Which brings us to two such contractors, Sarah and Mabel.

"Sarah came to me one afternoon and told me that Mabel's conduct did not reflect well on the company," Alexandra said. "Mabel was speaking ill of me, she wasn't paying attention to details, and customers were complaining. Apparently this had been going on for quite a while, and other contractors knew about Mabel's behavior, but no one was willing to tell me about it until Sarah did."

Alexandra had had some misgivings about Mabel for a while, so Sarah's story corroborated what Alexandra had suspected. Alexandra said to Mabel, "Some of our customers are complaining about the way you're comporting yourself at our functions. And I also understand that you're saying less-than-flattering things about me. Is this true?" Mabel nodded yes and apologized, but that was the end of her work for Culinary Architect Catering.

Sarah is one of the Good Ones. She had the strength of character to have a difficult conversation about a coworker with the boss. "I understand that no one wants to be a rat," Alexandra notes, "but I need to know if someone's behavior doesn't reflect well on the company." It wasn't easy for Sarah to blow the whistle, but it was the right thing to do. If she hadn't spoken up, the bad word-of-mouth Mabel generated would have continued, and who knows how much business Alexandra might have lost?

Courageous contractors like Sarah take their company's mission seriously and are willing to do what is necessary to honor that mission. Sarah is one of fifty people who work for Alexandra's company, but as a person of high character who isn't afraid to stand up for what she believes in, she's one in a million.

Courageous Men and Women Fight for the People They Work For

"She never conceded defeat on a book, and she never conceded that anyone who owed me money should be allowed to get away with it." That's the writer, economist, and actor Ben Stein talking about his literary agent, Lois Wallace, shortly after she died. In a moving eulogy he wrote for *The American Spectator,* Ben painted a picture of someone who had the courage to fight for her clients. A writer goes to great lengths to create a work that will enlighten, inspire, and entertain, but all that effort is for naught unless a literary agent can find the right publisher to produce and promote the book.

Here's an example of how Lois fought for Ben: "Last year, I had an idea for a book called *What Would Nixon Do?* about how RN would have handled the foreign policy crises of our era. With the help of John Coyne and Aram Bakshian, I submitted a lengthy proposal. She eagerly tried to sell it but she could not. Editors wanted things about personal finance from me and my genius writing partner, Phil DeMuth. No one wanted (so I learned) a defense of Richard Nixon. That did not stop her from trying."

That she was unsuccessful in her efforts isn't relevant. Whatever your line of work happens to be, there are lots of people out there who don't have faith in your product or service — or you. That's why discerning clients like Ben Stein want fighters like Lois Wallace on their team. They're willing to take on seemingly insurmountable challenges to advance the interests of the people they work for. That's why courage is one of the ten qualities of high-character employees and contractors like Lois.

"But wasn't it Lois's job to try to sell Ben's work?" you might ask. "Why should she be considered a high-character agent for doing what she was being paid to do?" It would be nice if the people who are supposed to look after our best interests always did what they should do, but that's not the world we live in. I know many writers who complain that their agents won't respond to emails, let alone work diligently to sell their books to publishers. Lois's fierce dedication to Ben is commendable.

Also, literary agents work strictly on commission. They take on only those projects they believe in or that they think are marketable (whether or not they personally like them). If an agent isn't on board with a writer's project, he or she won't represent it, even if the agent already represents the writer and even if the writer is a celebrity. Lois believed in Ben's book, and by extension, in Ben, even though the proposed work concerned an unpopular political figure. She fought a good fight on Ben's behalf, and that's why I consider her courageous.

Courageous people like Lois are among the Good Ones, and it's in an organization's interest to hire them, promote them, and fight for them the way they fight for their clients.

Courageous Employees Do Unpleasant but Necessary Things

No one likes confrontations. Some managers balk at having difficult conversations with employees, but the alternative — doing nothing — is worse. The problem persists or grows.

When an organization decides it needs to downsize, or when a board of directors chooses to fire the CEO, some ways of implementing these decisions are more honorable than others. George Zimmer, founder of the clothing company Men's Wearhouse, who was featured in ubiquitous TV commercials that guaranteed "You're gonna like the way you look," was let go from his company via email. Why? Probably because it was easier than having a face-to-face conversation.

There's a squirm-inducing scene in Jason Reitman's film *Up in the Air* that speaks to this. Ryan Bingham, a career-transitions consultant played by George Clooney, travels to St. Louis to fire people in person. The reactions of the fired employees feel authentic for a good reason: the director filmed men and women who had recently been laid off. Reitman told them to look into the camera, pretend it was the person who had fired them, and say the things they said or wished they'd said at the time.

Later, Bingham's company decides to cut costs by using videoconferencing to let people go. Bingham's younger colleague Natalie Keener, played by Anna Kendrick, is called upon to do the job, and although she is spared from having uncomfortable conversations in person, the virtual approach turns out to be hurtful for both the fired employees and Keener herself. There is no easy way to give unpleasant news — except by email, where you don't have to experience the consequences.

At least when I was fired from my high-school job at a fast-food restaurant in San Antonio, my boss had the decency to call me into his office and tell me directly. (That's the only honorable thing he did. I'll tell you more about him in the next chapter.)

Courageous Employees Ask for Help

Suicide wasn't the first thing Craig Kappmeier thought about after his wife left him and he lost his job with a major financial company. He didn't think about much of anything; depression kept most of his thoughts at bay. Eventually, however, the despair that enveloped Craig led him to consider taking his own life.

"Being fired for what I believed was no good reason would have been enough of a stressor on its own," Craig says. "The collapse of my marriage of eight years, on its own, would have packed a wallop, as would not being able to see my kids every day. But all three of them occurring at the same time? I fell into a deep depression for weeks." A devout Catholic, Craig believes that suicide is immoral, yet his future seemed so bleak that ending his life seemed like his only option.

"What stopped you from doing it?" I asked.

"Something within myself told me that I had to ask for help, right away," he said. "So I sent an email to 200 friends. In the subject line I put KAP NEEDS YOUR HELP. I wrote a detailed letter explaining what had happened to me. I asked them for three things: 1) to pray for me, 2) to offer advice for dealing with my situation, and 3) to let me know if there were any jobs they knew of that I could apply for."

Craig told me that 150 people opened the email, and 30 people responded.

> Several people said they would pray for me. A few asked me to send them my resume and they would forward it to the HR department where they worked. I appreciated every response I got. But it was one in particular that made me change my way of thinking. It said, 'Craig, you have three daughters who need you. Stop feeling sorry for yourself and get it together.' I immediately made an appointment to see a therapist and get to the bottom of who I was and what I needed to do to make some changes for the better.

Two years after reaching out to his friends, Craig has a job with a Fortune 100 company and feels better than he has in a long time. "I see my daughters every weekend, the people I work with are fantastic, and I feel more optimistic about the future than ever before."

Craig is the kind of employee that smart organizations want to have on their team. That seems like a strange statement to make about someone who was let go by his boss and his wife. I don't know how much these situations were a direct result of poor judgment on Craig's part. What I do know is that Craig had the courage to ask for help. This simple but difficult act saved his life, prompted some deep soul searching, and ultimately led to his becoming a stronger employee and a healthier, more responsible human being.

I asked Craig whether it was hard for him to reach out to his friends the way he did. "Of course," he replied. "I was afraid that they would see me as weak, or needy, or deeply flawed. But I also knew that if I didn't do it, I was going downhill fast. Ultimately, my faith prompted me to find the strength to keep going. Without that, I don't think I'd be here talking to you now. In fact, I'm sure I wouldn't be."

Employees Who Lack Courage Place Themselves and Their Companies at Risk

Dirk was a popular employee at a large consulting firm who started off as an accounting clerk. Because he was always willing to take on extra assignments, his supervisor asked him if he'd like to do some of the bank reconciliations. Dirk didn't have training in bookkeeping but jumped at the chance to move up. That was the beginning of a problem that would ultimately have dire consequences for both Dirk and his company.

Not long after Dirk started doing the bookkeeping assignment, he discovered he was out of his league. But instead of going to someone and getting help, he just changed the numbers and made them balance. The problem became compounded over time, because a few small changes led to big changes. Somehow Dirk was able keep this charade going for several years without anyone suspecting what was going on.

One day Dirk approached Oliver, a senior consultant, and confessed. Dirk felt terrible and said he knew he had to come to terms with his fraudulent activities. The firm spent a lot of money to get the matter straightened out, and Dirk was fired. People at every level of the company were shocked when the news came out. In fact, some people thought it was an unfounded rumor, since Dirk seemed like the last person to do such things.

Oliver told me that had Dirk found the strength early on to tell his supervisor that he was in over his head and needed help, the bank statements would have been reconciled properly, and Dirk would still be happily employed with the firm. But he lacked the courage to say, "I'm sorry, but I just can't do this work."

Such an admission would have been difficult to make. Perhaps Dirk felt he'd be letting his supervisor down. But as unpleasant as it surely would have been, what actually happened was far worse. The downside to saying "I can't handle this assignment" is a temporary loss of face. A sympathetic supervisor could have responded with, "I appreciate your letting me know. That couldn't have been easy for you to do, Dirk." Instead, Dirk wound up costing the company a small fortune, causing a lot of frustration and anger, and losing his job, all because he lacked the courage to be honest when he needed to be.

Obstacles to Courage

Fear of Being Fired

Stanley is one of the finest people I've ever known. His distinguished career as an accountant in both academics and business has spanned four decades, but a situation that occurred early in his professional life continues to haunt him.

In the mid-1970s, he worked for a family-owned company with $5 million per year in revenues. One day, the CEO, Wilbur, asked Stanley to run some personal expenses through the company accounts. Stanley resisted but was reluctant to stand up to his boss. "It was early in my career, and I had a family to take care of," Stanley said. Wilbur continued the practice, eventually costing the company $50,000 a year.

Stanley took meticulous notes of what was happening, in case the company got audited. It was, but the duplicity was never discovered. Stanley eventually couldn't endure being directed to violate both his conscience and the ethical standards of his profession. "It wore on me and was the biggest reason I ended up leaving the company," he told me.

I asked Stanley if he tried to get support from within the organization. "Yes, but I got nowhere with that. The general business manager told me to go along with Wilbur's demands." He added, "The owner was also chair of the board, and the attorney on the board was the owner's adviser." This dire scenario recalls Gary Cooper's going it alone in Fred Zinneman's film *High Noon*. If, unlike that Western hero, Stanley wasn't able to rise to the challenge at the time, he certainly gained a valuable lesson from it. We can understand Stanley's reluctance to tell Wilbur, "I can't do what you're asking me to do," even if we wish he had been able to find the courage to do so.

"The problem with Enron, WorldCom, Tyco, and the other business scandals of the early oos wasn't just the bad leadership in those companies," says Bill Treasurer, a former member of the U.S. high-diving team and author of *Courage Goes to Work*. "People who knew about what was going on didn't speak up. It was for understandable reasons — fear of retaliation — but then you find those occasional people like Sherron Watkins or Cynthia Cooper or Colleen Rowley at the FBI who have enough principle to put something of themselves at stake to do the right thing, which is hardly ever the easy thing."

Fear of Bodily Harm

Simone Stewart is director of her own consultancy firm in Kabul, which helps to launch brands in the Afghan market and offers advice about business contracts to U.S. forces and other NATO members. In her previous job, she discovered that her employer, a food service company, was selling alcohol illegally.

"My father was a member of the Training Team, a specialist unit of the Australian Army that operated during the Vietnam

War," Simone told me via Skype, "and he instilled in me a desire to fight for what you believe in and to never be swayed by other people's agendas or to look the other way." She discovered that the company was allowing alcohol to be supplied to a member of the Afghan underworld, who sold it on the local market. By doing so, the organization was putting its own employees at risk by engaging in illegal war racketeering. Simone felt she had no choice but to blow the whistle on her own boss. After several months of collecting evidence, she contacted external auditors, who exposed the irregularities. The people involved were fired.

The company's once-dominant presence in Afghanistan became severely diminished, as a report from the Center for Public Integrity detailed. Simone knew that being a whistleblower, particularly in a war-torn part of the world, carried risks, but she wasn't prepared for the death threats that followed. To protect herself, Simone left Afghanistan for several years. But she realized she had fallen in love with both the culture and its people and felt that she could continue to make a positive contribution to the efforts to rebuild Afghanistan, so she returned. She no longer has to deal with dishonest employers, because now she runs her own business, and she calls the shots. "In spite of all the risks, I would do it all over again," she says. "There is just no way I could have lived with myself had I turned a blind eye to what was going on. That's not the kind of person I am."

Could you have done what Simone did? I can imagine how troubling it would be to discover that my employer was engaging in unfair business practices that endangered my fellow employees and me. It's remarkable that Simone was willing to go back to a place where she had truly dangerous enemies. "Some people have called me the Erin Brockovich of Afghanistan," Simone says with a laugh. She is one of the Good Ones for having the strength of character to stand up to wrongdoing. And yet I can see why others in a similar position would choose not to risk their lives for what is right.

Fear of Damaging a Relationship

What are the two most important rules in life? "Work hard and strive to be happy"? "Help people and take care of yourself"? "Live simply and share the wealth"? According to Jimmy Conway, the gangster Robert De Niro portrayed in Martin Scorsese's *GoodFellas*, it's none of these things. "Never rat on your friends," he tells young wannabe crook Henry Hill. "And always keep your mouth shut."

Minding your own business may be good advice for people in Hill's line of work (if you don't want to die of very sudden, acute lead poisoning). We saw how speaking out threatened Simone Stewart. There are times, however, when the consequences of *not* speaking out can be severe. Consider the people in Elvis Presley's inner circle, some of whom were employees of his company and were known as the Memphis Mafia. After the King's divorce from Priscilla Presley in 1973, his drug habit spiraled out of control. Bass player Norbert Putnam was disturbed by what he saw in December of that year during recording sessions at Stax Studios in Memphis. "Someone should have staged an intervention, and that someone was Tom Parker," says Putnam, referring to Elvis's manager. "But he didn't, and I wish I knew why." Putnam adds that an intervention might not have worked. He notes that Red West, Elvis's bodyguard and a member of the Memphis Mafia, "always had Elvis' back and I think he tried to do something. But no one could get through to him with all of that medication."

We'll never know if a concerted effort would have worked. In

1977, the greatest rock-and-roll artist of all time died alone in his home at the age of forty-two from complications of drug abuse.

In spite of the fear of damaging valued relationships, some employees do speak out when it's necessary, and the results are impressive. Lori, an administrative assistant in a financial services company, had to make a tough choice during her first job:

> One of my duties was processing invoices from sales, marketing, and other departments. A mid-level manager in sales — I'll call him Don — gave me an invoice for $1,500 for hats and T-shirts for his department's softball team. But the company's policy was that the players had to pay for their own uniforms. I told Don I couldn't do what he was asking. He was surprised — he probably thought that since I'm nice to everyone and had just been at the company for six months that I'd be a pushover. We'd also developed a friendship at work — nothing romantic. I stood my ground, and he never asked me to do anything like that again.

I asked Lori if this was an easy or hard decision for her to make. "I knew it would be wrong to process Don's invoice, but at the same time, I worried about how standing up to him would affect our relationship. I suppose he thought I'd go to HR and report him. Maybe I should have, but I didn't. I didn't sleep well the night before I decided to tell him 'no.' Our relationship was never the same after that."

Had Lori chosen to submit the invoice, we can appreciate why: it would be difficult to stand up to a person at work who has more power than she did and who had become a friend. But even though such a move would be understandable, it can't be justified.

Lori is one of the Good Ones because she chose to do what was right, rather than what was easy. Had members of the Memphis Mafia done the same thing, who knows how much longer

Elvis would have lived, and how many more albums and performances the world could have enjoyed?

Fear of Humiliation

John A. Byrne has a distinguished career in journalism. He has been the editor in chief of *Fast Company* magazine, *Bloomberg Businessweek* online, and now C-Change Media, a digital media company that has developed prominent websites for business school students, executives, and others. He is in his early sixties now, but a situation he encountered when he was eighteen challenged his ability to take a stand against a workplace bully and ultimately changed the path his life would take.

When John was a freshman in college, he worked at the school's newspaper. "One of the top editors — I'll call him Basil — used his power and influence to get what he wanted, even when it wasn't best for the paper," John said. "He would dominate every meeting, making all the core editorial decisions about who should do what and which stories ended up in the paper."

Basil made life difficult for everyone who worked there, and John wanted to stand up to him and tell him to stop it. But Basil was an extrovert, and John is shy. "I was afraid he might kick me off the paper if I didn't have any support. I also worried that he could diminish me intellectually in front of my colleagues, whose respect I wanted."

Eventually John had had enough and confronted Basil at a meeting. Basil was shocked. "I don't think anyone had ever stood up to him before. He didn't fire me, and the others at the paper thought what I did was great," John says with a lift in his voice. The experience gave John a huge boost in self-confidence. "I really don't believe I would be the person I am now, or would have accomplished all of the things I have in journalism, had I not had the courage to stand up for what I believed in."

Speaking truth to power is a valiant act, yet as John's story illus-trates, the fear of humiliation can hamstring anyone. I've known John for years and have always thought of him as a supremely confident (but not arrogant) person. I never would have guessed he was ever unsure of himself. Those days are over for him, for good.

Fear That Nothing Good Will Result

May is a bartender at a high-end restaurant. She noticed that her colleague Randy had a policy of pouring drinks for friends with-out charging them, a clear violation of the restaurant's policy. "I felt that if I didn't take action of some sort, I would be guilty by association."

"But you didn't do anything wrong yourself," I replied.

"Yes, but the independent company that monitors alcohol use and revenue had flagged us for not having income consistent with the amount of liquor we'd dispensed. For all I knew, they might have thought *I* was the person giving away drinks. Besides, Randy was stealing from the company that had been good to us. He was costing the company at least $100 a night in uncollected reve-nue. On a five-night work schedule, that's $500 a week, $2,000 a month, $24,000 a year."

The first time May observed what Randy was doing, she called him on it, but he laughed it off. She then reported the incident to her manager. May got nowhere with him, so she worked her way up the hierarchy until she spoke with the restaurant owner.

No one did anything for months. One of the managers was friends with Randy and stood by his buddy. When the monitoring company's additional investigation made Randy's actions impos-sible to deny, the company told him he could no longer tend bar in the establishment. But they kept him on as an employee and made him a server in the restaurant. This was hardly the negative repercussion that May expected.

Believing that your efforts won't be successful is a compelling reason to avoid speaking out about wrongdoing at work. Finding the strength to be brave is hard enough. But what if you do what needs to be done and the change you seek doesn't occur? In May's case, the owner of the business thanked her for what she did, but Randy was merely reprimanded. He wasn't fired, he wasn't suspended, and he didn't have to pay the restaurant back for the drinks he gave away. His job just shifted from the bar to the dining room.

May broke down in tears when she described the toll that all of this was taking on her. "This job pays well, and I need the income, but I can't put up with how corrupt this place is."

"Do you regret blowing the whistle, since the injustice wasn't rectified?" I asked. She didn't miss a beat. "Not at all. I'd do it all over again if I could. My grandmother taught me to treat others fairly, and I had witnessed unfair behavior on the job. I had to speak up." Confronting dishonorable behavior is its own reward. Sometimes it's the only reward.

Are Courageous Employees a Threat?

One can imagine a manager balking at hiring a person who demonstrated courage in a previous job. "Why would I want to bring someone on board who has a history of standing up to people?" he or she might say. "A person who doesn't mind standing up to an authority figure might take issue with *me* somewhere down the road. Who needs the hassle?"

Recall the story of Marvin, a fire safety director who refused to take a bribe from a vendor of fire extinguishers. He told that vendor in no uncertain terms that Marvin's company would no longer do business with him if he continued to make dishonest offers. Isn't it possible, or even likely, that a future employer would view Marvin as a troublemaker? Why would a company risk losing business by hiring a guy like him?

I asked Marvin's former colleague Ken Meyer why an employer would hire someone like Marvin who makes waves. "You *want* an employee to make noise," Ken responded animatedly. "High-character people like Marvin drive your business by looking for ways to make things better. And they're not doing it because it benefits them. They're doing it because it benefits the organization. *That's* what drives them."

In the short run, Marvin could have cost the company money. In response to his refusal to acquiesce in corrupt behavior, the vendor might have said, "Ah, that company is too much of a headache to deal with. I'll take my business elsewhere." Then Marvin's company would have had to go to the trouble of finding a new (and honest) vendor of fire extinguishers — but at least they could have been sure that their fire extinguishers were in working order. Taking a long-range view when evaluating employees like Marvin makes it clear why he is one of the Good Ones. Having an employee who is willing to stand up to corruption, avoid risking human life, and reduce the company's legal liability are three compelling reasons for bringing courageous people like Marvin on board and promoting them once they're there.

Evaluating Courage

Questions for Job Applicants

The first two questions are courtesy of Bill Treasurer, founder of Giant Leap Consulting, Inc., and author of *Courage Goes to Work*.

Describe a time when you had to disagree with someone in authority and stand your ground. What was the situation? How did the other person react? What did you do?

Bill says managers who ask these questions should pay attention to how the respondents portray themselves. An authentic response will probably include a reference to vulnerability. Courage, Bill notes, isn't the absence of fear; fear goes hand in hand with doing courageous things. Standing up to someone in a position of authority or influence, as Marvin did with the dishonest vendor, would be frightening for a lot of people.

In *The One-Minute Manager*, Ken Blanchard and Spencer Johnson present the "praise down/criticize up" model of management. This upends the traditional arrangement in which direct reports extol the virtues of their bosses, and bosses have the freedom to find fault with their direct reports. Blanchard and Johnson say that if companies are to succeed, their leaders must welcome disagreement, even — or especially — from their subordinates.

The corrupt fire-extinguisher salesman was Marvin's boss in the sense that companies are beholden to suppliers as well as to clients: no supplies, no business. Marvin criticized up and stood his ground, and now his story is repeated in the company's orientation sessions.

Ken Meyer noted that Marvin stood his ground with the vendor not because Marvin was stubborn or wanted to feel powerful, but because he believed that what the vendor was asking him to do was wrong and could have lethal consequences. That's courage at its best, and a job candidate who has done something along these lines is, like Marvin, one of the Good Ones.

Tell me about a time when a direct report pushed back on you and felt strongly about a position. What was the situation? What did they say, and how did you react?

This question, Bill says, aims to get a sense of the type of leader the candidate is. Does he or she invite people to speak their minds? It takes a strong leader to admit to the possibility that he or she is mistaken or hasn't thought a matter through thoroughly enough. "McKinsey & Company is one company that prides itself on constructive disagreement," Bill notes, adding that in his experience this is a rare trait in corporate culture.

The best leaders, Bill observes, welcome principled push-back. "They don't want to be surrounded by sycophants and yes people. Otherwise, they'll be closed off from the good information they need to make good decisions. That's why they do well to listen to people who have enough backbone to resist going along with dunderheaded ideas." Having less power and authority may *explain* why direct reports don't always speak up when something bothers them. But that doesn't *justify* the practice.

Tell me about a time when you needed to take a stand but didn't. What got in the way? What effect did the experience have on you?

It's been forty years since Stanley's boss ordered him to run personal expenses through the company accounts, but Stanley has never forgotten about it, and it prompted him to renew his commitment to standing up for what he believes in. In the "Obstacles to Courage" section above, we looked at some of the factors that can discourage someone from doing what needs to be done.

A meaningful response to this question would include one or more of these limiting factors. It might also include a story about how the respondent ultimately took a stand later on. The stories we considered with respect to each of these obstacles are models of what an authentic answer might look and sound like.

SUMMARY

Courageous employees

- tell managers things they need to know
- fight for their clients

- do unpleasant but necessary things
- ask for help

Fears of being humiliated, being fired, and damaging valued relationships are significant but surmountable obstacles to being courageous at work.

CHAPTER 5

FAIRNESS

The N word is ugly. It's racist. What would you do if you were on the receiving end of it? David Dawit Searles was nine years old when a neighborhood kid named Billy used it against him. No one had ever done that to David before. He was hurt and confused, but he refused to respond with more hatred. His mother told him, "Be a fixer, not a destroyer."

A few weeks later, David had the chance to be just that. Billy was walking his dog near where David was playing when all of a sudden the dog broke free from Billy and ran into the street. That street was a major thoroughfare in Washington, DC, and cars were coming from both directions. David ran after the dog, grabbed him, and prevented him from being killed. David risked his life to save his neighbor's pet, and from that moment, he and Billy became best friends.

Fifty years later, David was working as a sound engineer at a major cable news network. He was putting a lapel microphone on a guest, an influential national politician I'll call Senator Smith, when the senator noticed that the previous guest was someone from the other predominant political party (let's call him Representative Jones). "Check the trash can for bombs!" Senator Smith said in all seriousness. "I don't trust that guy. Who let him in here?"

"Sir, excuse me, I don't think this gentleman would do something like that," David responded. "In fact, I belong to that man's party, so I don't take that very kindly." The politician was stunned. Then he mumbled, "Oh, well, I didn't mean it that way."

One of the reasons David said he spoke up is that Representative Jones is African American. Senator Smith's comment thus had worrisome implications, both political and racial. The senator was being unfair, and David felt he had to stand up to him. David could have lost his job for confronting a guest, but that thought didn't enter his mind. He remained at the network for four more years and then moved on to a competitor.

Because of David's commitment to fairness, he is one of the Good Ones. That both of his stories also involve courage is a further testament to David's integrity and illustrates how the qualities of high-character employees can overlap.

In my previous book *Ethical Intelligence*, I explained that fairness has three major applications at work: allocating scarce resources appropriately, especially time; disciplining people in the right way; and turning unjust situations into just ones (as with David's response to Senator Smith). Fairness is also an important consideration in hiring, deciding on raises and promotions, and making job assignments. When these endeavors are carried out by fair managers, good things happen both to the employees on the receiving end and to the organization itself.

What Is Fairness?

To be fair is to give to others their due. Fairness is sometimes discussed in terms of justice. Fair employees have a commitment to justice, especially economic justice (paying employees fairly), social justice (ensuring that the rights of employees, such as freedom from discrimination, are respected), and procedural justice (resolving disputes). Let's now consider, in practical terms, what it means for high-character employees to be fair.

Hiring

Leo is senior vice president for communications at a large bank in the Northeast. Last spring, he and his direct reports, Brian and Cheryl, reviewed the applications for a coveted summer internship in the department. The internships are paid positions. Student interns are offered full-time employment after graduation, and the starting pay and benefits are highly desirable. But there's only one slot each summer for a communications intern, and last year the department received an unusually high number of résumés.

Leo commented, "There sure are a lot of weird names this time." Brian replied, "Yeah. A lot of Asian names. Indian too. Arab. Aren't there any regular Americans in the group?"

Cheryl was disturbed by this conversation. Brian seemed unaware that India is an Asian country or that everyone applying for an internship was an American citizen. But Cheryl knew that the bank had also hired interns who were German, British, and Australian nationals in previous years, and Brian had never had a problem with those students. Most of all, though, Cheryl didn't like the language her coworker and boss used to describe the applicants. But she didn't say anything, because she doesn't like confrontations.

Leo, Brian, and Cheryl set up brief interviews with the top seven students, based on their GPAs, previous internship experiences, and the quality of their cover letters. Six of the students had Chinese, Korean, or Indian surnames. One student, Mitch, had an Anglo-Saxon last name. It was a hard choice — all of the candidates did well in their interviews — but it was Mitch who was offered and accepted the internship.

During Mitch's internship, Cheryl was bothered by the way the department had selected him. Mitch did a good job with the limited responsibilities that interns have, but Cheryl wondered if he was chosen because he truly was the strongest candidate or for less honorable reasons.

This spring, Leo, Brian, and Cheryl were once again reviewing the internship applications, which were almost double the number from the previous year. All but two had surnames that were not Anglo-Saxon. When Leo and Brian again commented on the ethnicity of the applicants, this time Cheryl spoke up.

"Is this a KKK rally or a business meeting?" she asked. She said it half jokingly to soften it a bit, but Leo and Brian didn't think it was funny.

"I'm not racist," Brian said angrily. "I'm just commenting about their names. When did you become so PC all of a sudden?"

"Yeah, last time I checked, this is still America, and we have the right to free speech," Leo added.

"I'm not saying you don't have a right to say what you're saying. I just don't think it's right, that's all," Cheryl replied.

Leo rolled his eyes, Brian shook his head, and they proceeded to debate who should get invited for an interview. Of the three students short-listed after the interviews, one was Caucasian, and two were not. As Leo, Brian, and Cheryl discussed the pluses and minuses of each, Cheryl wondered if her own bias had played a role in who had made it this far and who should get the internship.

"I did my best to focus on the merits of each candidate," Cheryl told me. "I'm not sure I did that last year, even though I don't consider myself to be prejudiced." Cheryl lobbied hard for a finalist named Kimiko, based on Kimiko's strong work ethic and cheerful personality.

"Do you want her because you really think she's the best, or because her name doesn't sound like yours or mine?" Brian asked her. "I could accuse *you* of being racist."

Leo stepped in. "I agree with Cheryl. Kimiko is the best one of the three."

Cheryl was surprised to hear that. She wondered if maybe Leo had had second thoughts about the possible role of race in the selection process. It could also be that he agreed with her that Kimiko was the strongest candidate. Kimiko got the internship.

Is it legal for employers to talk and act the way that Cheryl, Leo, and Brian did? Is it fair? B. David Joffe, an employment-law expert and a partner with Bradley Arant Boult Cummings LLP in Nashville, is troubled by the previous story. "An employer may not legitimately base an employment decision on an employee's foreign accent, nor can an employer legitimately make an employment decision based on an applicant's name," David notes. "When the employer decides to interview only candidates with names that sound like 'regular Americans,' the employer is impermissibly taking national origin into account." That would violate Title VII of the 1964 Civil Rights Act, which prohibits discrimination on the basis of national origin (as well as sex, race, and other classifications).

But even before President Lyndon Johnson signed the act into law, it still would have been wrong for Brian, Leo, and Cheryl to take a job candidate's national origin or race into their deliberations, or to make jokes about it. Just because a practice hasn't (yet) been ruled illegal doesn't mean it's right, or fair, or honorable. Tina Turner asked, "What's love got to do with it?" Listening to the bank employees' discussion, Tina might pose another question: "What's race got to do with it?" The only thing that should matter about a potential employee or intern is whether he or she can do the job well.

Unfair employment decisions are thus dishonorable and potentially costly. Overlooking job applicants because they have accents or because their grandparents were born in other countries is wrong for both reasons. David told me that "if discriminatory hiring practices are proven, Title VII establishes that damages as high as $300,000 can be awarded to the plaintiff." State laws may provide for additional redress. Alan Tecktiel has seen additional fallout in cases like this, including class-action lawsuits and brand damage that is difficult to repair.

It is legitimate for employers to verify a candidate's eligibility to work. A person's national origin or the sound of his or her name are not within these bounds. The legal and responsible way for employers to avoid an expensive day in court is to make a conscious effort to consider only those factors that are relevant for the work at hand and then select the person who best meets those criteria.

Raises and Promotions

Carlee was a senior manager at a large accounting firm in Philadelphia. The firm's stated policy was that compensation is based on merit. Carlee, a strong performer, had seen increases in her bonuses each year. Sam, Carlee's direct report, was also a strong performer, and he had received excellent reviews for the past five years, but he had never had a raise or an increase in his bonuses, even though he had requested them numerous times. He had not even seen a cost-of-living increase in salary. Carlee appealed to HR several times to get Sam a raise, but each time she was told that he was at the highest pay grade for his job assignment.

Carlee believed that the company was not treating Sam fairly, so she lobbied HR one more time. This time she got a response she hadn't heard before. "The only way for Sam to get a raise is for him to get a promotion," an HR manager told Carlee. But the only position he could be promoted to was Carlee's, which she didn't want to relinquish.

Carlee talked with her own supervisor, Hiroshi, about Sam's situation. Hiroshi too believed Sam was owed a raise, but Hiroshi's efforts on Sam's behalf were not successful, either.

"What if we split my position so Sam would be my peer instead of my direct report?" Carlee asked Hiroshi. "Would that work? I could focus on our U.S. clients, and Sam could handle the international ones. As long as I don't have to take a pay cut, I think it would be a fair solution. Given the HR policy here, it's really the only solution." Hiroshi had never heard of such a thing happening at the company, but he liked the idea. He proposed it to HR, and after several months of negotiations, Carlee's proposal became a reality. Sam's new salary and next bonuses reflected his considerable achievements, a result consistent with the firm's stated policy on compensation.

Carlee is one of the Good Ones, because an injustice occurring on her watch bothered her to the point that she fought for a change, even though it meant relinquishing some of her own power. But when I presented this case to Syd, an HR manager, he objected to my conclusion. "This story doesn't seem real," he claimed. "Carlee's idea is admirable, but the company is now paying more for essentially no extra value. And Sam's initial situation does not qualify as an injustice. There is no evidence that he was paid unfairly for the job he was in. He simply was topped out."

I asked Carlee what she thought about Syd's concerns. "The firm *is* getting more bang for its buck," she told me, "because Sam is able to focus on an aspect of our business that had been in my purview. I was able to handle both our domestic and international accounts adequately before, but now each side has a senior manager dedicated to its interests, and everyone is better off this way."

But what about Syd's criticism that the company had been

treating Sam fairly all along? "That's not true," Carlee objected. "Sam was performing well year after year and was able to devote more and more skill to the job. But he didn't see any corresponding increase in his rewards from the company. Sam was not being paid according to his merits before. Now he is." I'll say it again: Carlee is one of the Good Ones!

Ken Meyer, the HR vice president who told me about Marvin, says that Carlee is exactly the kind of high-character employee that companies should have in their ranks. He told me another story about Daphna, an employee at his organization. Like Carlee, Daphna couldn't stand the idea of an injustice going uncorrected.

"During a routine review of compensation reports, Daphna noticed that a staff member got a degree and was entitled to a pay raise," Ken said. "The staffer reported the degree a year and a half ago, but nothing happened. Daphna said, 'This is wrong. We have to make it right.'" She made sure that the employee got the raise and that it was retroactive to the point when he got his degree.

Ken has heard of too many cases where an employee overdue for a raise did not get the back pay that Daphna fought for. "You want your people who find a mistake to make it right. And that comes from the desire to make things right."

Making Job Assignments Fairly

Juan was the president of an organization where I worked many years ago. Juan loved his work and had a passion for serving his clients, and I never saw him in a bad mood. He was the first person I thought of when I decided to discuss giving assignments.

Some of my friends in the business world used to complain that their bosses played favorites, giving the best assignments to the employees they liked best (who in many cases were also the most attractive ones in the department). Those friends rightly felt passed over, and their bosses' behavior did nothing to boost employee morale, except among those who had been given special treatment. This wasn't unfortunate: it was unfair. Juan did just the opposite. He made assignments based on how well the employee's abilities fit the task at hand. Employees got assignments appropriate to their knowledge, skills, and experience. The same was true for everyone else at the company.

Over the years I've heard a lot of people say things like, "I'm not racist. I'm not sexist. I don't judge people on the basis of their looks or politics. I see people for who they really are." Juan was one person who truly was like this.

Juan was far from perfect. He had a short temper. His attention didn't linger on anyone or anything for very long. He required employees to go to his house every summer for team-building exercises that were intended to be fun but were often excruciating. Some of us called these excursions "forced fun." But that's as bad as things ever got. Whatever problems we had to face in our jobs, unfair work assignments weren't among them.

Having favorite employees isn't necessarily unfair or dishonorable. Barbara Moses, the author of *Dish: Midlife Women Tell the Truth about Work, Relationships, and the Rest of Life*, notes that sometimes favoritism "isn't capricious or driven by the boss's ego needs — it is based on talent." The favored person "is simply more skilled, or has more potential. Or the manager is more comfortable with that employee because of a compatible work style." In Juan's organization, for example, there was an employee I'll call Emmett who had many business contacts. Like Juan, he was what Malcolm Gladwell, the author of *The Tipping Point*, calls a "connector." If Emmett got more high-profile assignments than the rest of us, it was because of his extensive network. Juan's decisions weren't unfair, because Emmett was one of the highest performers in the company.

The criminal-justice system has the saying, "The punishment should fit the crime." In business, when it comes to assigning employees to projects, the saying should be, "The project should fit the employee."

Obstacles to Fairness

Unconscious Bias

The first thing you notice about Jack Welker, the white supremacist played by Michael Bowen in the TV series *Breaking Bad*, is the big black swastika on his neck. Jack makes no bones about his racism. You've heard of people wearing their hearts on their sleeves? Jack wears his hatred just below his head.

Jack Welker is hardly one of the Good Ones. But not everyone who is racially prejudiced flaunts a tattoo with a Nazi symbol. What about the person who passionately proclaims, "I don't judge people by the color of their skin. I don't care if a person is black, white, yellow, or purple — I don't think of people in terms of their race"? Can we be sure that that person always lives up to this ideal?

The problem has to do with *unconscious* bias: prejudice that flies below the radar of one's awareness. As Don Feldmann, CEO of Rippe & Kingston Capital Advisors, Inc., in Cincinnati, notes, however, it's possible to be aware of the effects of such bias. "If I'm bothered by something that a job candidate has done, I pay attention to this feeling, but I then ask myself, 'OK, what's really going on here? Do I feel this way because of something that's genuinely wrong with the candidate, or is it my bias?' Sometimes your instincts are valid, and sometimes they're not. It's a hard call. We're capable of fooling ourselves a lot."

Kirk LaPointe, executive director of the Organization of News Ombudsmen and editor in chief of Self-Counsel Press in

Canada, speaks of "situated knowledge" as a limit to what interviewers are able to see when they evaluate job candidates. The term, coined by Donna Haraway, a scholar of science and feminism, refers to the biases that come from the way we grew up, our socioeconomic status, race, gender, and other factors. "Journalism isn't objective," Kirk notes, "and neither is the job interviewing process. You can't completely eliminate your biases," he says, "but by being aware of what they are or might be, you can avoid getting caught up in them." One executive told me that when he is interviewing job candidates, he makes two columns in his notes. "Column one is what I actually heard, and column two is my judgment," he says. This technique gives him a reality check against the biases he may have.

When Brian and Leo made comments about the racial backgrounds of some of the internship applicants, Cheryl was upset. And although she doesn't consider herself prejudiced, she wondered if she herself might be unconsciously favoring people who do *not* have Anglo-Saxon names. The reason why unconscious biases are so troubling is that we're not aware of them.

When I hear someone say that he or she doesn't pay attention to a person's race, I'm glad to know that that person rejects racism, but I'm not convinced it's possible or desirable to avoid noticing the color of a person's skin (at least if you're blessed with the gift of vision). The issue isn't whether we notice how others differ from us — of course we do. The issue is what we do with that information.

There are biases other than racism that can also limit a person's ability to hire and promote employees fairly. Do you think the world would be a better place if everyone thought and acted the way you do? I'll admit I sometimes feel this way. But the world would be a dull place if it were populated by people with identical appearances and points of view. Consider Ira Levin's novel *The Stepford Wives,* in which a town's male residents conspire to replace their wives with humanoid robots who are all programmed to obey their husbands. They don't have an original thought in their heads, because they're not human.

If you do harbor the conscious or unconscious wish that other people should think and behave more like you, your evaluation of a present or future employee will be shaped by the degree to which the person shares your values, preferences, and beliefs. That bias might adversely affect how you evaluate a job candidate or current employee whose worldview differs from yours.

Suppose, for example, that you're interviewing two people, Justin and Larry, for a position. Both appear to be strong candidates. But suppose also that Justin has an accent, or is short, or has some other attribute that for whatever reason you don't like. How can you be certain that your bias against people with that attribute won't get in the way of your evaluation of Justin?

Perhaps the song "Everyone's a Little Bit Racist," from the satirical musical *Avenue Q* has the right idea. I have biases, and so do you, and it's better to accept that fact than to pretend it's not true. (It's better still, of course, to work on minimizing their impact or getting rid of them altogether.) High-character employees in managerial positions, like Don Feldmann and Kirk LaPointe, do their best to be aware of their biases, and they're willing to question the decisions they make about whom to bring onto the team and whom to let go. It is right and good for people who are charged with hiring and promoting sometimes to get another point of view before they proceed, which may correct unconscious bias and unfair decisionmaking.

Self-Interest

To be fair is to be impartial. It's therefore hard to hire or promote someone fairly if you have something to gain or lose from the decision. Chris Webb, the founder and CEO of Ready for Duty Haul-Off Construction in Burleson, Texas, learned this the hard way when he hired his son to be a part of the construction crew.

"The construction industry, particularly at the largely unregulated residential level, has changed very little since Jesus worked for Joseph as a carpenter," Chris told me. The people who own construction companies pass their skills down to their sons and daughters, who are then expected to take over one day. Chris was proud to bring his son Matt into his successful company. But Matt had a difficult time viewing his father as the boss.

Chris became increasingly frustrated with his son's unwillingness to view Chris as the boss rather than as Dad. "Matt, you work for me," Chris told his son.

"No, I work *with* you, and you should treat me with more respect," Matt replied.

"I treat you exactly the way I treat the other men who work for me. How do you want me to treat you?" asked Chris.

"Like your son," Matt answered.

Eventually Chris fired Matt. "That saying, 'Don't mix business with pleasure,' has a broader truth: 'Don't mix business with family,'" Chris says. Hiring his own son burnished Chris's fatherly pride but wound up impeding the construction crew's effectiveness. Matt is a good man, but he wasn't the right man for the job.

Ultimately, Chris and Matt were able to work out their differences. "After a year of starving, suffering through low-paying jobs with worse bosses than me, and growing up a bit, Matt became more willing to accept me as his boss," Chris says. Everybody won: Chris got a good employee and regained his paternal pride, Matt got a good job, and the company continued to serve the needs of its customers.

Chris's story had a happy ending but remains a cautionary

tale. A hiring decision based on self-interest may not be fair to other job candidates, to the employees who work with the new hire, or to the company's clients.

Evaluating Fairness

Of the ten crucial qualities of high-character employees that we're exploring in this book, fairness is among the most difficult to evaluate in job candidates. The questions below are a modest attempt at breaking through this barrier.

What are your biases?

Why not just come straight out with it? As we considered in the previous section, all of us have biases. They may not be on the level of *Breaking Bad*'s neo-Nazis, but they're there.

The problem with this question is that it all but begs the interview subject to lie. What person who seriously wants a job or promotion will be specific about his or her prejudices, should they even be aware of them in the first place?

Still, some answers are better than others. A round of applause goes to the interviewee who speaks of having reflected on this subject already and how he or she has worked to overcome their limitations. Recall how Don Feldmann questions why he feels the way he does about a job candidate, pro or con. Merely considering the possibility of his own biases helps him to do the best job he can in evaluating a candidate fairly.

Tell me about a time when you were discriminated against. How did it affect you, and what did you do as a result?

In the story that opened this chapter, we saw how David Dawit Searles dealt with a neighbor who used the N word against him when the two were kids. After David risked his life to save the neighbor's dog, the two became friends. That experience, along with his upbringing, prompted him to speak out when he encountered an injustice at work many years later.

Apple's CEO, Tim Cook, talks about a formative experience growing up in a small town in Alabama. Riding his bike on his way home, Tim saw a burning cross on the lawn of a family he knew was African American. A group of Klansmen stood there, shouting racial epithets. After he heard a window break on the house, Tim yelled, "Stop!" A man in the group removed his hood, revealing himself to be a deacon at the local church. "This image was permanently imprinted in my brain, and it would change my life forever," he said in a speech, and went on to talk about how human rights and dignity matter. Apple, he says, is dedicated to "advancing humanity," and to that end, he recently became the first CEO of a Fortune 500 company to identify publicly as gay. "If hearing that the CEO of Apple is gay can help someone struggling to come to terms with who he or she is, or bring comfort to anyone who feels alone, or inspire people to insist on their equality, then it's worth the trade-off with my own privacy," he wrote in *Bloomberg Businessweek*.

How would a high-character person talk about what he or she learned after being unfairly discriminated against? Here are some possible responses:

"The experience gave me an insight into prejudice that I didn't have before."
"It made me want to make sure that I never treated anyone like that myself."
"It's one of the major reasons I went into this line of work."

If I were answering this question, I would talk about how I had been fired for no good reason when I was working at a fast-food restaurant in high school. The job of cashier required making a note of every twenty-dollar bill we received. One busy

Sunday morning when I was working the cash register, I received a lot more twenties than usual. At one point, I wasn't sure if I'd noted the twenty I'd just been handed, so I made a note of it, which turned out to be a mistake. The register thus said I'd taken in twenty-one bills when I'd really taken in only twenty, and the next day the manager accused me of having pocketed it. He fired me on the spot.

Being fired for any reason is stressful, but when it's unjustified, it's hard to describe the sense of indignity one experiences. Granted, it's not on the level of being sentenced to prison for a crime one didn't commit, but it's still unjust. And I believe it played some role in my decision to write and teach about ethics for a living. (It also led me to a much more rewarding job and a transformative encounter with a humble woman named Emily, whom I'll talk about in chapter 7.)

Fair Employees: Help or Hindrance?

Why would an employer want to hire someone like David Dawit Searles, whom some might view as a loose canon, ready to confront anyone when he perceives political or racial insensitivity? Do we really want employees to feel free to take action whenever they feel an injustice is taking place at work? I asked David these questions, and here's what he said: "Without people standing up to injustice, you'll have people undermining you, and you'll have cutthroat activities. The key to speaking up isn't just what you say; it's how you say it. When I spoke to that U.S. senator, I tried to be as dignified as I could, and I didn't show any anger. I just called him on something that shouldn't take place here."

One of the reasons people like that senator feel free to shoot their mouths off is because no one is willing to confront them, to say, "That's not right." It takes courage to be able to do that, but even before courage, it takes the ability to recognize an injustice.

SUMMARY

To be fair is to give to others their due.

High-character employees strive to be fair at work regarding hiring, raises and promotions, and job assignments.

Interviewer bias is an obstacle to fair hiring but can be managed successfully.

Hiring and promoting fair employees can reduce or eliminate the legal and financial troubles that arise from unfair business practices.

CHAPTER 6

GRATITUDE

When I started counting my blessings, my whole life turned around.
—Willie Nelson

After speaking to members of the business community in Novi, Michigan, on the topic of ethical intelligence, I handed out small square stickers imprinted with the five points of my talk. A week later I received a card in the mail from a woman who had been in the audience. The front of the card showed a roadside billboard with rolling hills in the background, and on the billboard itself was a photograph of my sticker!

I did a double-take and thought, "This is the most amazing card I've received in years." Christine Harkins Reid, a local businesswoman who was in the audience, had designed it for me. The card contained not only an elegant thank-you note but also a packet of flower seeds that Christine said symbolized the work I do as a professional ethics speaker. To go to such lengths and create a unique way of expressing gratitude touched my heart and made me smile.

It impressed me so much that I contacted Christine to find

out how she was able to put such a distinctive thank-you note together so quickly. She told me about a company she works for that allows people to write notes on their computers, personalize them with whatever images they wish, select small presents like flower seeds or gift cards to include, and have the company print and mail them. She had scanned the sticker I'd given to her, placed the scanned image on a stock photo, and written a note using a font that mimics handwriting. For years I'd been meaning to send thank-you notes on a regular basis but had never gotten around to doing it. The service made it easy, so I signed up for a monthly subscription, without even a soft sell from Christine. Her expression of gratitude gave her a new client and benefited both people she knows (me) and people she doesn't know (namely the clients I now send thank-you cards to).

The purpose of this chapter is to reveal why gratitude isn't merely a nicety of doing business. It's a powerful character trait, and although it's hard to discern, it's worth looking for in prospective and current employees. Through their generosity of spirit, grateful employees benefit clients, colleagues, and the business itself. They're more satisfied, more productive, and nicer to be around. Can a business prosper if the people who work for it aren't in the habit of expressing gratitude? Perhaps. But a group of people on a mission is more likely to flourish when its members realize how much they owe to one another and take the time to acknowledge this sincerely, kindly, and regularly. It's time to recognize how important gratitude is in the life of an organization and to the people who practice it.

What Is Gratitude?

Gratitude is both a way of looking at the world and a way of acting in it. Grateful people recognize several things:

- We have many bounties in our lives.
- We depend on one another for these bounties.
- It's good to express our gratitude to others for how they've helped us.
- When we acknowledge their help, our benefactors feel better, and so do we.
- When we feel good, we tend to be more productive.

As with the other character traits we examine here, gratitude means more than expressing appreciation only once in a while. If Margie, your direct report, thanks you only on your birthday for the many things you've done to help her, she can't be considered a grateful person with respect to your relationship with her. Margie may think highly of you and feel like a valued member of the team, but if she keeps these thoughts and feelings to herself, she's missing an opportunity for making a good relationship even better.

Let's look more closely at the five elements of gratitude described above.

We Have Many Bounties in Our Lives

One of my favorite books is *The Berenstain Bears Get the Gimmies,* by Stan and Jan Berenstain. It's a kids' book, but it has a lot to do with business life.

Brother and Sister Bear are cubs who want what they want when they want it. Candy, toys, you name it: if they see something that appeals to them, they demand, "Gimme!" Their parents, Momma and Papa Bear, realize they need to teach their offspring the value of moderating the compulsion to want more. The cubs also need to appreciate what they already have.

Eventually Brother and Sister learn what Mick Jagger told us years ago: you can't always get what you want. The cubs come to realize that it's fine to want things, but it's also a good idea to look around and recognize the bounties we too easily take for granted.

But how did we get those bounties in the first place? It's tempting to think they come strictly through our own efforts, but that's not true.

We Depend on One Another for Bounties

I'm writing these words on a notebook computer, and I can't imagine how many people were responsible for inventing this indispensable tool. Even if I were using a pen and a pad of paper, it would be hard to estimate how many men and women played a role in designing, producing, and distributing them. The same is true for whatever you're using to read or listen to these words — a hardcover or paperback book, an e-reader, or a digital audio player. You're able to do this only because of the hard work of hundreds, perhaps thousands of people. And all of this applies just to my act of writing and your act of reading or listening. It's mind-boggling to think of how many others are involved in everything else we do — driving to our jobs, working in an environment protected from the elements, using furniture, eating lunch. Even if your business is manufacturing, you probably don't produce every component of the things you make.

No one is an island, as John Donne recognized almost four hundred years ago. The intimate characters that Dolly Parton and Kenny Rogers portray in the song "Islands in the Stream" surely recognize that beyond their romance, they're connected to and dependent on more people than they know, just as you and I are.

It's Good to Express Our Gratitude to Others for Enriching Our Lives

After Robin Williams died in 2014, many of his colleagues and friends told reporters how much they had benefited from their relationships with him. The same thing happened after the death of Philip Seymour Hoffman a few months earlier. You can count on it happening again later this week, or today, when another prominent person passes away. But I always wonder, "Did these people ever tell their colleague or friend these lovely words when that person was still alive?"

We all know folks whose bosses are horrible, and in subsequent chapters we'll hear about several of them. Some of our friends complain about their nasty coworkers. At an airport recently I saw the best-ever title for a business book: *People Can't Drive You Crazy If You Don't Give Them the Keys,* written by Mike Bechtle. But do those of us who are blessed to work with and for good people express our gratitude for this blessing? High-character employees do, and everyone benefits from this practice.

Grateful Employees Are More Satisfied

Robert Emmons, a professor of psychology at the University of California, Davis, has done extensive research documenting the psychological and physiological benefits of practicing gratitude. Emmons has shown that compared with people who don't do this regularly, grateful people sleep better, live longer, and are more satisfied with their lives. They're less likely to suffer from depression, phobias, drug and alcohol dependency, and premature heart disease. "Grateful people report higher levels of positive emotions, life satisfaction, vitality, optimism and lower levels of depression and stress," Emmons says.

The physical benefits of gratitude mean that it is in an employer's financial interest to hire grateful people. They are less likely to miss work and run up the business's health insurance premiums. From an employer's point of view, the physical and emotional benefits make gratitude a very desirable trait in job candidates.

Christine Harkins Reid, who sent me the personalized thank-you card, gets tangible benefits from her practice of expressing gratitude. She develops ongoing relationships with many of the people she sends the cards to, and some of those recipients, like me, become clients. What started out as a fun side project blossomed into a full-time business, which enabled Christine to leave her previous job and create a career based on saying "thank you" every day.

"Practicing gratitude in the moment of frustration can really be a game changer," a senior HR manager told me. "I had an employee who made a lot of mistakes and talked too much. My annoyance with him grew. But one day, when I felt myself getting irritable, I decided to think about what I appreciated about him. From then on, I made sure to think about his positive contributions instead of the bothersome things he did. It totally changed how I treated him, which ultimately helped him perform better."

People on the receiving end of gratitude benefit, too. For Christine's colleagues and friends, there are the immediate pleasures of her thoughtful, personally designed notes, along with whatever goodies she has included (such as books, gift cards, or brownies). But some recipients, like me, also derive long-term benefits. Partly because of her gesture, I've developed a daily practice of expressing gratitude, and I believe this is one of the main reasons I've been feeling so good for the past several years. Along with health, meaningful relationships, and a sense of purpose, gratitude plays an important part in a life well lived.

Gratitude Promotes Productivity

Grateful employees do more than make others feel good and retain customers: they get more done. A study by Margaret Greenberg and Dana Arakawa at the University of Pennsylvania suggests that grateful managers may promote productivity. The researchers looked at how managers from an information technology organization treated the people on their teams. One of the metrics in the study was recognition, an aspect of gratitude. Employees were asked to agree or disagree with statements like, "My project manager recognizes my accomplishments regularly" and "I know that my project manager will recognize my hard work/devotion." Greenberg and Arakawa found a positive correlation between managers who regularly recognized the work of employees and project performance. A study by Robert Emmons and Michael E. McCullough showed that people who kept gratitude lists were more likely to achieve professional and personal goals.

The experiences of a mid-level financial manager I'll call Naomi validate these findings. The most important thing for Naomi at work is feeling that she makes a difference. She used to work at a company where her supervisors never complimented or thanked her, even though she often went above and beyond the call of duty. They paid her well, and she had benefits like health insurance and paid vacation, but for Naomi it was a thankless job, and after a while, she found herself not wanting to do much more than what was required of her.

Because she prides herself on exceeding expectations, when she noticed she wasn't motivated to give the job her all, she left. She realized that she needs to work with people who value what she does. At the business where she works now, she feels so appreciated that she volunteers for projects like running an international seminar series for the marketing team. It's time-consuming, but everyone from the most senior managers to the speakers she hires for the seminars lets her know how much they value what she does. This is one of the main reasons why Naomi routinely does more than her employers require of her.

It's astounding how something that takes such little effort and money can yield such powerful dividends. Naomi does great work for her firm in part because she has a strong work ethic, but also because the people she works for acknowledge her efforts and thank her. While researching this book, I heard more than one executive say that regular but informal recognition like a heartfelt "thank you" is far more powerful than formal reward and recognition programs.

Ingratitude Hurts Companies

In 2012, the American Psychological Association surveyed over 1,700 employees and found that over half of them were looking for new jobs because they didn't feel appreciated. This is a tragedy. Naomi's previous employer lost an intelligent and productive employee quite needlessly. Had Naomi's boss simply expressed his gratitude for Naomi's hard work from time to time, she might still be working there, and the institution wouldn't have had to go to the considerable trouble of looking for a replacement.

An episode of the AMC series *Mad Men* is a perfect illustration of this situation. Peggy Olson, a woman who has worked her way up from the secretarial pool to the top ranks of the advertising world, tells her mentor, Don Draper, that she feels unappreciated, but Don is far from sympathetic.

> Don: It's your job. I give you money, you give me ideas.
> Peggy: And you never say thank you.
> Don (*angrily*): That's what the money is for!

Don misses the point. What Peggy, Naomi, and other underappreciated employees want is not to be pampered or flattered. They want to feel as though they matter. And because they do matter, the people who manage them would do well to acknowledge this fact.

Obstacles to Gratitude

If gratitude is such an important quality to have, why is it so hard to cultivate and express? What gets in the way of gratitude in the workplace?

Gratitude Is Hard to Express

Expressing gratitude makes us vulnerable. When Raj, one of the people who works for you, thanks you for something you have done on his behalf, the power imbalance that naturally exists in the manager–direct report relationship is amplified. Raj is implicitly acknowledging that he needs your help. The reality, of course, is that we're all indebted to one another. But particularly in the United States, where we have long viewed success as a matter of individual struggle and personal achievement, it's not easy to accept the ideas of interconnectedness and mutual dependency.

Acknowledging what others do for us may feel, for some, like a weakness or even a character flaw. Many cultures value the notion of pulling yourself up by your bootstraps. According to this way of thinking, all you need to become successful is will-power. Gratitude requires you to acknowledge that you *cannot* succeed alone, and this may feel like a form of failure.

Gender may also play a role. Sean, a senior editor at a publishing company in New York, told me, "I think it's particularly difficult for a man to admit to being vulnerable, especially if his boss is a woman." Research by Todd B. Kashdan, Anjali Mishra, William E. Breen, and Jeffrey J. Froh, published in the *Journal of Personality,* suggests that Sean is onto something. In several studies they conducted at George Mason University and Hofstra University, the authors discovered that "men were less likely to feel and express gratitude, made more critical evaluations of gratitude, and derived fewer benefits" than women did. It would be worth exploring how barriers to feeling and expressing gratitude could be overcome, as the authors themselves conclude. Simply being aware of these barriers is a good place to start.

Cultural Differences May Play a Role

Val Wright, a corporate consultant who has worked with Amazon, BMW, and other leading companies, told me about how a jazz concert led to a valuable "Aha!" moment for her:

> Earlier this year I took my mother to a local jazz club to hear Jane Monheit, one of my favorite artists. During the performance, my mom seemed confused, and I couldn't figure out why. It turns out that she didn't understand why the audience would applaud after each musician's solo while the rest of the band was still playing the tune. She was accustomed to going to classical concerts where the applause happens only at the end of each piece. Once I explained to her how audiences at jazz concerts respond to performances, and why this is considered appropriate conduct, she was transformed from a confused observer to an engaged participant!

Val experienced some disorientation herself when she moved to the United States, and her experiences have something to teach us about the relationship between gratitude and culture. Born and raised in England, Val's first job was in the HR department of the Xbox video-game division of Microsoft there. She now works in Los Angeles. "Two of the things that shocked me about corporate life in the U.S. are how often praise is given and how effusive that praise is," Val told me. "In England, you're praised at work when you do something of great magnitude, such as going far beyond what you're expected to do. When I moved here, it seemed as though I was hearing 'Well done!' proffered for the simplest tasks."

Should we conclude from Val's experiences that gratitude is valued more in the United States than in the United Kingdom? Or that both cultures value gratitude but express it differently? There is some evidence to support the latter idea. Research by Blaire Morgan, Liz Gulliford, and Kristján Kristjánsson at the University of Birmingham suggests the two cultures differ in how gratitude is understood and expressed. Morgan and her colleagues note that although it would be a mistake to speak in stereotypes of the "cynical Brit" and the "American optimist," they provide empirical evidence that may indicate the U.S. and the U.K. think differently about what it means to be grateful.

Research by World at Work, a nonprofit human resources association based in Scottsdale, Arizona, suggests that cultural differences regarding gratitude extend beyond the transatlantic gap. According to a recent survey of the association's members, who represent companies such as Del Monte, Eli Lilly, and Google and nonprofit organizations such as the American Red Cross and National Geographic, fewer than half of the groups' international employees participated in all or most of the same recognition programs as North American employees.

These cultural differences have potent implications for hiring and promoting employees. "If your organization places a premium on frequent expressions of gratitude, it's important to let potential employees know this," says Val Wright. "You could say to an applicant, 'We expect employees to express gratitude to the people who help them at all levels: direct reports, colleagues, and supervisors. *How* you do it is up to you. But *that* you need to do it is not. If this isn't something you're comfortable with, this wouldn't be a good fit.'" Joel Manby, of Herschend Family Entertainment, makes it clear to job candidates that the company is based on seven ethical standards, and gratitude plays a central role. "This is our ethos," he tells applicants. "If you love it, come work here." He advises people who don't subscribe to those standards to look for work elsewhere.

It's not difficult for managers to tailor the expression of

gratitude to the needs and wishes of team members. Alan Tecktiel asks each employee he manages to write on an index card whether they want to be thanked and if so, how (publicly or privately). "I save these in their file and memorize them so I can thank them in the way that they most value," he says. Granted, this technique works best with relatively small teams, and it requires a good memory, but with some creative thinking, expressions of gratitude can be customized in any organization.

Although there are good reasons to hire and promote grateful people, it behooves organizations to determine what gratitude means to them and to hire people who share that point of view. One can imagine some companies saying, "We show our gratitude to our employees by paying them, and our employees show their gratitude to us by doing their jobs well. Nothing beyond that is expected." For companies that do place a premium on expressing gratitude, however, it makes sense to bring up the topic during the interview. Better to find out there that an applicant isn't comfortable giving or receiving thanks on a regular basis than to have to deal later with an employee who doesn't share one of the fundamental values of the organization.

Would it be catastrophic to hire such people? No. Does it make sense to minimize the possibility for interpersonal tension in the workplace by hiring grateful people if gratitude is an important value in a company? Yes.

The Belief That Gratitude Should Flow in Only One Direction

"Gratitude greases the wheels of business," said Sean, the editor. "I've worked here for over twenty-seven years and have trained lots of people, but I very rarely hear people thank me for helping them to become a good editor or to develop skills they can take with them wherever they go. And I've noticed that employees in their twenties are especially reluctant to express gratitude to me."

I've known Sean for a long time, and I've never considered him to be a complainer or a particularly needy person, so I was surprised by his comment.

Sean's belief that gratitude should flow both ways in an organization — from senior to junior employee and from junior to senior — is contrary to much of the thinking in management. Earlier I referred to the "praise down/criticize up" rule of management from Blanchard and Johnson's *One-Minute Manager*. I like the authors' call for powerful people to express their appreciation. When Carol, a senior manager, makes a habit of thanking her direct report Meg for the good work she does, everyone wins: Meg gets the praise she deserves (and the positive feelings that go along with it), clients benefit from Meg's good work, and Carol promotes and maintains a strong relationship with a valued employee.

Yet it also behooves Meg to thank her boss, whose leadership allows Meg to flourish. If Carol is like Sean, she'll appreciate the acknowledgment. If Carol is like Val Wright's colleagues from the United Kingdom, all she has to do is say, "Your good work is all the thanks I need. But I appreciate the gesture."

Evaluating Gratitude in Job Applicants and Employees

The Grateful Job Applicant

Gratitude in job applicants is not easily quantifiable, but it can be assessed. Because there are many nuances associated with this character trait, we'll take a different evaluative approach from that used in other chapters by considering two interview scenarios. Helen is the HR manager of a large clothing company, and Adriana and Mirabel are two women applying for a position in Helen's department. Looking closely at Helen's conversations with these candidates will help us discern small but significant differences in how grateful Adriana and Mirabel are in their professional lives.

A<small>DRIANA</small>

Helen: Adriana, I see you've been a human resources manager for a long time.

Adriana: Well, I've been doing it so long that when I started, it was still called "personnel"! (*laughs*)

Helen: And you were president of the local chapter of the Society for Human Resource Management a few years ago. What made you want to do that?

Adriana: When I was starting out in HR, I joined the chapter, and the president at the time made a point of welcoming me to the group and called me from time to time to see how I was doing. No one in the previous jobs I'd had ever did that, and it made me want to get more involved. I started volunteering for various committees like membership and education, and eventually someone suggested that I run for president, since she said that people liked working with me. I didn't really have that ambition, and I was concerned about the time commitment, but it turned out to be one of the best things I've ever done. I remembered how grateful I was when the president reached out to me years ago, so I made it a point to do the same thing for our new members.

Helen: What are you proudest of having accomplished during your year as president?

Adriana: That's a tough one. I'd have to say that our members really enjoyed the programs we put together, and although I can't claim full credit for that, I will say that I invested a lot of time looking for fun topics and engaging speakers. We were one of the first chapters in the country to use Pinterest and Facebook as marketing tools, and they helped me find presenters who I thought could make our monthly meetings enjoyable. And it was one of our newer members who had suggested that we use these tools and correctly predicted how important they would be.

MIRABEL

Helen: Mirabel, you have an impressive résumé.

Mirabel: Thank you. I've worked really hard in every job I've ever had.

Helen: What achievement are you proudest of?

Mirabel: That's hard to say. A lot of people liked the article I wrote for our trade magazine on how HR managers can use social media successfully. In fact, that article led to a couple of national TV interviews, and one of the producers told me I was a great guest and that she'd definitely invite me back.

Helen: I remember that article. What prompted you to write it?

Mirabel: Well, I'm just surprised by how often people put things on Facebook and Instagram that could embarrass their employers and that don't do their own reputations much good. I'm on a mission to make this a top issue in HR, and I've got my work cut out for me. I've had accounts with Facebook, Twitter, and LinkedIn since before most people had ever heard of them, and I'm more aware of the potential downsides than anyone I know. I keep up with the changes, so I'm pretty much the go-to person for social media.

Helen: You're really passionate, I can tell! What do you like so much about HR?

Mirabel: I've had other jobs, but I until I got into HR, I always felt like a little fish in a big pond. It's nice to finally be recognized for what I know and can do. I mean, I was the nerd in high school who was always playing video games and designing websites. I was kind of an outsider back then, but the things that made me a geek at the time are now in high demand.

Helen: Do you consider yourself a team player?

Mirabel: Yes, but I find that too many people lack a strong work ethic. I expect a lot of the people I work with, just as I expect a lot of myself. Too often I end up doing most of the tasks no one else wants to do. But I enjoy working with others, and I'd like to think they enjoy working with me.

On the face of it, both Adriana and Mirabel seem like they'd be good additions to an HR department. They're accomplished, knowledgeable, and passionate. There are subtle but important differences, however, that are worth noting. Adriana lets Helen know that other people have played an important role in her success, and her ego doesn't get in the way of giving them credit. Although she used the word *grateful* only once, it's clear that gratitude plays a strong role in her life.

Mirabel also refers to other people, but only in terms of how they make her feel. You don't get the sense from Mirabel that her achievements had anything to do with anyone but herself. Even self-described nerds like Mirabel owe at least some of their technical expertise to others. Of course, Mirabel wants to impress Helen with her accomplishments, but because those accomplishments were made possible by the contributions of other people, a truly impressive candidate would note that with a grateful heart. There are no self-made women or men.

It's also troubling to hear Mirabel disparage her teammates. She may indeed have had the misfortune of working with a few slackers, but surely she has also had colleagues who have helped her, just as she helped them. Why, then, doesn't she mention them?

Evaluating a job applicant's practice of gratitude requires going beyond the interview and looking for things like the way an applicant treats the person at the front desk and others who aren't directly involved in the interviewing process, and whether he or

she sends a thank-you note after the interview. Assessing gratitude in someone you don't know is trickier than assessing things
like sales performance and professionalism, but it's a worthwhile
pursuit.

It's much easier to consider how grateful a person is after he
or she has worked at the organization for a while; the 360-degree
review we discussed in the introduction is a helpful way to add to
what a manager knows about an employee directly.

Is Ingratitude Enough to Nix an Applicant or Employee?

Suppose that George is applying to work for Paul's organization,
and Ringo is up for a promotion. Both George and Ringo are
highly knowledgeable and skilled people. George, by all counts,
would make a terrific employee, and Ringo has already demonstrated that he is. But both men have a problem: they don't exhibit
the character trait of gratitude. George doesn't write Paul a
thank-you note after his job interview, and in the seven years Paul
has known Ringo, Paul has never seen him display any evidence
of being a grateful employee. Is this single shortcoming sufficient
to deny employment to George or advancement to Ringo?

No. Of the ten crucial traits associated with high-character
employees, the most expendable might be gratitude. George and
Ringo's abundant positive qualities make up for their failure to be
thankful — and imagine how useful they'll be when Paul needs
a band for the company holiday party. But "the problem is that
when an employee is weak in the gratitude department, they tend
to be lacking in other areas as well," says Kevin Kennemer, CEO
of the Tulsa-based consulting firm the People Group. In Kevin's
experience, an ungrateful employee is often someone who doesn't
have a strong work ethic and thus doesn't take accountability seriously. I've also seen that the converse is true: grateful employees

are more likely to work hard and be loyal to their organizations. And an example of this is Kevin himself.

I met Kevin two years ago, when he hired me to give a talk to the Oklahoma Business Ethics Consortium during the year he served as its president, and he was a joy to work with: gracious as well as grateful, generous with his time, and committed to making sure that the speakers he brought in had everything they needed. He met me at the airport when I arrived, which clients rarely do for speakers. For Kevin, being grateful comes as naturally as looking after the people he works with and for.

Kevin stands in sharp contrast to another client I'll call Marlon. When I worked with Marlon on a couple of speaking engagements, not once did he ever say "thank you," let alone express any recognition that I was giving my all to ensure a successful event. Perhaps he thought, as Don Draper did, that paying me was the only thanks I needed. But his unwillingness to express any appreciation for the service I provided was matched by shortcomings in other areas: he delegated work on the engagements that he should have done himself; he frequently missed appointments we'd made; and he mismanaged some of the logistics of the talks. I was well compensated for the work I did, but some things are worth more than money. Working with gracious, grateful people is high on that list for me. I can't wait to work with Kevin again. If Marlon invites me back, however, I'll pass.

SUMMARY

Employees who are grateful are more productive and satisfied than employees who are not.

There are cultural differences in how gratitude is offered and psychological reasons why gratitude is difficult to express.

Gratitude is most beneficial when it flows in both directions: from managers to team members and back again.

CHAPTER 7

HUMILITY

Remember when soft drinks came in glass bottles? Even though they were heavy to lug around, the glass didn't alter the taste of the soda the way that plastic bottles can. They also looked cool.

When Janice Piacente was the chief risk and compliance officer for a global beverage company, she was faced with a knotty problem: how to get the phone number for the company's ethics and compliance hotline in front of everyone who worked there. Putting it on posters scattered throughout offices around the world made it too easy to overlook, so that serious violations of corporate policies might go unreported. What would make the number unmissable?

That's when Janice remembered the glass bottles her company used to make on a wide scale. The bottles are still available, but they're much rarer and therefore much more desirable: they're collector's items. What if the phone number were printed on a sleeve that covered the glass bottle? Wouldn't that make the phone number something every employee would *want* to have around?

Her idea was met with great acclaim, and it soon became the company's method for distributing its hotline number. Employees loved it. Janice brought a bottle with her when she gave speeches to other compliance officers, who shared the problem of how to get employees to take compliance seriously. The answer, Janice showed, is in branding the compliance office so that its message is recognizable and even fun. Audience members were so impressed that they came up after her talk and took pictures of the bottle with their smartphones.

Janice is proud of her achievement, but she refused to take the credit for it. Instead, she gave the credit to her team. "I just had the idea for it," she says, "but my team implemented it. They made the bottles. They designed the artwork. They made my idea a reality." Janice doesn't deny that she played a role in the development of the innovative item. But when she talks about the project's success, she places the emphasis on the *team's* effort. "The focus is on 'we,' not 'me,'" as she puts it.

Janice is one of the Good Ones because she is the embodiment of the humble employee. For Janice, recognizing the contributions that her team makes to accomplishments like the hotline on a bottle is right for its own sake. But her humility has the wonderful side effect of motivating her team to give her their all. "They work as hard as they can, because they don't want to disappoint me," she says. "My number one job is to help the people who work for me be successful."

I asked how Janice came to develop this view. "I once had a boss who loved to say, 'Rank has its privileges,'" she responded. "It bothered me a lot, and I swore I'd never treat people like that."

Humility is one of the ten crucial qualities of employees of high character, and smart businesses seek out people with humility to work for them. These employees inspire their coworkers, instill confidence in their supervisors, and move up quickly in their organizations.

What Is Humility?

There's a lot of misunderstanding about what humility is. The Oxford Dictionaries website defines humility as "a modest or low view of one's own importance." No wonder, then, that some people have a low view of humility itself. "Humility is not a virtue," a blog for hipsters claims. "Underestimating your abilities is just as dishonest as overstating them."

If the commonsense understanding of humility is correct, then it would be bizarre to consider this to be a quality of high-character employees. Do we really want businesses to be populated by meek, self-denying people? Think about the title character in *Annie Hall,* played by Diane Keaton. For much of the story, Annie is nervous, unsure of herself, and constantly second-guessing her decisions. It's a comedy, but a workplace made up of Annie Halls would be closer to a nightmare.

But humility shouldn't be regarded as a low view of one's importance. It is, rather, an *accurate* view of it. It's a view of oneself that is based on reality, rather than the distortion that occurs when we look at ourselves uncritically or through the fog of our own ego.

We can all do without coworkers who take the credit when a project is successful. On the face of it, this behavior simply seems rude. It's not polite to blow your own horn, we're taught. Let others praise you. Keep your victories to yourself.

The problem, however, isn't that such coworkers are impolite: it's that they're *mistaken.* As we saw in the chapter on gratitude, we don't accomplish great things all by ourselves. We have help every step of the way. Some of that help is behind the scenes, but it is help nevertheless.

Consider the mountain climber who reaches a summit alone. You can hear the cry of "Yay me!" No doubt the climber is to be commended. He or she has probably trained for months or years, overcome tremendous physical and psychological obstacles through sheer force of will, and achieved something that many people only dream about.

But who made the backpack, boots, and weatherproof clothes the climber is wearing? Didn't the climber get encouragement from friends and family, some of whom probably had to make some sacrifices on the climber's behalf (such as staying home and paying the bills or providing child care)? And the fact that the climber is alive in the first place has nothing to do with the climber and everything to do with his or her parents. Our climber has every reason to be proud of having the physical and mental strength to ascend to the mountaintop. But he or she also has good reason to recognize and appreciate the role that others played in this achievement.

David J. Bobb, founding director of the Hillsdale College Kirby Center for Constitutional Studies and Citizenship in Washington, DC, explains why humility seems an unlikely component of success:

> It's not easy at first glance to see how humility could ever lead to greatness. Humility hardly seems that good, let alone great. Implying something lacking — a loss of strength or a sapping of vitality — humility often strikes modern individuals as something to be avoided. Observed superficially, humility can appear weak and passive — anything but great. Greatness seems strong and energetic — anything but humble. "It's hard to be

humble," Muhammad Ali is reported to have said, "when you're as great as I am."

In his book *Humility,* Bobb shows how this character trait was essential to the achievements of Jesus, Socrates, George Washington, Abigail Adams, Abraham Lincoln, and Frederick Douglass. Humility is also a close cousin of gratitude.

Humility and Gratitude: What's the Connection?

When Janice Piacente gave the credit to others for implementing her idea for using soda bottles, I suggested that she was being humble. But isn't this an example of gratitude, not humility? It's both, actually. People express their humility through gratitude. By publicly recognizing her team's efforts in bringing her idea to fruition, Janice was saying, in effect, "The branded bottles could not have become a reality without the hard work and dedication of others." That's Janice's humility speaking. "And because I depended on them for making my idea a reality, I'm deeply thankful." That's the gratitude piece.

About love and marriage, Frank Sinatra sang, "You can't have one without the other." The same is true of humility and gratitude. Now we'll consider what humble people have to offer an organization.

The Professor Who Went to Prison

Most men and women who earn a PhD in philosophy remain in the academy, moving from one side of the lectern to the other. Gregory Sadler took a different route. He went to prison — to teach.

As a new faculty member at Ball State University in Indiana, Greg was invited to offer introductory courses in religious studies and philosophy at a maximum-security prison. In addition to books about Aristotle, Saint Augustine, and Martin Heidegger, Greg brought with him something troubling. "I came into the prison as a professor who had, and still has, serious anger problems," he told me. "Anger, its control and expression, and humility are actually connected with each other. We get angry when we feel that someone else is doing something wrong."

One of the things that irritated Greg early in his career was being challenged by the students he taught in prison. Greg believed he had all the answers. Who were students to question his wisdom? He even got into clashes with some of them, which, given the setting, "seems like a stupid place to do so, no?" he says.

Greg's work at the Indiana State Prison prompted him to look at his own life and some of the problems he had. "It would have been quite possible several times for me to be right where they were — having committed terrible acts and being stuck paying for it," he observes. Over time, Greg learned not to take things personally and to see that whatever was going on with an argumentative student was really more about the student than about him. "That sort of thing helps to put one's own role into perspective and helped to make me less of an angry guy."

Greg's experiences in the prison taught him humility in a less direct way, too. Some of his colleagues had a condescending attitude toward his career choices. They asked, "When will you be teaching for real?" Others sincerely congratulated Greg for doing what they believed was charity work. At first, Greg was angered by these attitudes. He had taken on the prison assignment not because he couldn't get a job teaching philosophy in an academic setting or because he thought teaching inmates was a noble or charitable thing to do. Rather, he believed— and still believes — in the potential of philosophy to enhance the lives of everyone, not just young people with the good fortune to attend college. The philosophy professors who believed Greg was cooling his heels until a meaningful appointment came along "thought too highly of themselves, their talent, and, most importantly, which students deserved them," he notes. When Greg understood that this attitude is rooted in hubris, the opposite of humility, he felt happier, less anxious, and less angry — and yes, more humble.

No company wants employees who will fly off the handle at the slightest provocation. But how can an organization increase the chances of having employees who aren't prone to angry outbursts? Hiring people who, like Greg Sadler, strive to be humble, is a good first step.

Humble Employees Benefit Their Organizations — and Themselves

"A man's got to know his limitations," says Dirty Harry in *Magnum Force*. But you don't have to be Clint Eastwood to see how crucial it is to understand what you *can't* do. Ana Cristina Reymundo, of American Airlines' *Nexos* magazine, believes that the most valuable employees are those who can recognize and acknowledge their limitations.

"My job as an editor requires me to give criticism on a regular basis," she says. "My goal is not to impose my own voice on a writer's work but to enable the writer's own voice to be expressed as clearly as possible. You can't get a consistently good product otherwise. But that usually means suggesting changes to the work, and some people handle those suggestions better than others. The writers who do it well tend to be humble people."

In chapter 4, I suggested that courage enables employees to accept constructive criticism, which ultimately benefits both the organization and the employees themselves. Courageous employees recognize that it's worth taking the painful step of acknowledging shortcomings. But as Ana Cristina rightly observes, accepting criticism requires humility as well as courage. "You have to remove your ego just enough to be able to step back and look at your work as it is and how it could become stronger." She told me about Jana, a writer who had done great work for other publications but had never written a piece for American Airlines before.

> When she turned her first piece in, it had a very different angle than I was expecting. Normally I might consider accepting the kind of submission Jana had made, but for the issue the piece was for, it just wouldn't work. I spoke with her and told her about the problem. She didn't get defensive. In fact, she was worried that I was disappointed in her. I told her that wasn't the case, gave her a set of actionable points, and even extended the deadline a little. She did the rewrite immediately and beat the deadline. We have a really nice and open dialogue. She takes instruction very well, and she has moved up very quickly. She started out with short movie reviews and has now done two cover stories, all in the space of two years. And I've sent her on international trips representing American Airlines, which is something I rarely allow.

I asked Ana Cristina to what degree humility contributed to Jana's rapid rise in the organization. "Completely," she replied, "because her humility allows her to be teachable, and that willingness to learn makes her a valuable asset to us." Jana's humility as a writer made her receptive to criticism, which gave rise to excellent work. But it has also created a strong bond with her boss: "Her openness instilled confidence in me," says Ana Cristina, which ultimately helped the magazine and Jana herself. Jana is one of the Good Ones, and her humility is a major reason why this is so.

Humble Employees Acknowledge Their Debt to Others

Janice Piacente was humble in giving credit to her team for implementing an idea she had, but she told me that the idea didn't come out of thin air. "We met with the chief compliance officer from Lego, the Danish company. They came to my office, and their business card is a little Lego man. They make little Lego men that kind of resemble you — like this guy was bald and had glasses, and this little Lego guy was bald and had glasses, and his name, phone number and email address were on the back of it. His business card was a Lego doll. How cool is that?"

Janice's idea for using a glass soft drink bottle with the compliance department's hotline number on it grew out of an encounter she'd had with a colleague at another company with a unique style of branding. Janice therefore gives credit both to her team, which implemented her idea, and to her counterpart, who showed her a novel way of getting a message out there. Janice's take on her accomplishment is not based on a low view of herself, as some dictionary definitions of humility would have it. It is based on an accurate view of herself as part of a web of connections.

The Humble Employee Is a Servant

The word *servant* has a bad rap. When I interviewed Jonathan Taplin, who produced Martin Scorsese's early film *Mean Streets* before the director was widely known and acclaimed, I asked him, "When you were looking for your first film to produce, was it that you wanted to work with Mr. Scorsese, or that the script appealed to you, or something else?"

"I wanted to work with Marty," Jon replied. "My work from the very beginning, when I started working with Bob Dylan and the Band, was always based on the artist. I would find somebody that I thought was brilliant and then do what I could to support them. That's the way I've approached things, and it's still pretty much the way I approach things."

In *Give and Take*, Adam Grant shows that people whose lives are devoted to giving to others are more successful than those who are primarily out for themselves or looking for a return on the investment of their effort. The givers Adam presents, including a writer who played a major role in making *The Simpsons* the longest-running program on television, are the kind of people Robert Greenleaf talks about in *Servant Leadership*. Adam's givers and Robert's servant-leaders focus on using their knowledge and skills to help other people. And both givers and servant-leaders are, at their core, humble human beings.

Jonathan Taplin is now director of the Annenberg Innovation Lab at the University of Southern California Annenberg School for Communication and Journalism, but he still sees himself as a servant. "I try to surround myself with the best and the brightest minds that I can find and then try and build a superstructure that can support their work." Jon is a giver and a servant. That's why he's one of the Good Ones — and successful.

When Employees Lack Humility

If humility is a crucial quality of high-character employees, what happens when it is in short supply? Some of the consequences may include the following.

Damage to One's Reputation

To illustrate my previous point about the tremendous effort it can take to hold people accountable, I talked about how I took a deadbeat client to court. My friend, an attorney named Richard Solomon, took on my case, and we prevailed in court.

After we won, I thought that the local news media might be interested in the ironic story of a well-respected New York institution (my former client) breaking its promise to pay a speaker who delivered a talk on ethics. I envisioned a video crew following the marshal delivering a court order to the school and getting footage that would be the lead story on the evening news.

When I proposed the idea to Rich, he immediately rejected it with a simple response that continues to inspire me: "Humble in victory, gracious in defeat." The court's decision in our favor, Rich said, was the vindication I had sought. There was no reason to rub it in the client's face. It would have disgraced the client, and I shudder to think what it would have done to my reputation as the Ethics Guy.

Rich is one of the Good Ones because he taught me the importance of being humble when you triumph. Rich's gentle lesson in the virtue of humility is something I take with me to work every day.

Being Passed Over for Jobs

Before he produced *America's Most Wanted* and became the executive in charge of its production company, Roger Chiang was responsible for hiring 250 people for Bill Clinton's 1996 reelection campaign. "Working on a presidential campaign is prestigious, and everyone wants the bragging rights of having worked for the president of the United States," Roger said. "A lot of the résumés I got were from the sons and daughters of influential people who had donated money or had political affiliations with the president."

A fellow whom I'll call Brett didn't make the cut because of his sense of entitlement and lack of humility. "He thought he could travel around in a motorcade and be close to the principals rather than do the work," Roger told me. That work wasn't glamorous and involved doing labor-intensive tasks like setting up campaign rallies. Brett's mother was a state legislator, and through his family, Brett knew both President Clinton and Vice President Al Gore. In spite of Brett's pedigree, however, Roger didn't bring him onto the team. "Whenever I hire or promote someone, I ask myself, 'Will this person be a good representative of the company, of the cause, of the culture?'" Roger says. Brett was not.

At the beginning of this book, I suggested that superior knowledge and skills may be *necessary* to be a leading job candidate, but they're not *sufficient*. Humility is another crucial quality of successful applicants.

Having Difficulty Accepting Helpful Criticism

Screenwriters who want to make their scripts as good as they can be sometimes hire Robert McKee, whose three-day seminars on the art and craft of screenwriting are legendary. You'd think that writers would listen to what McKee has to say after they spend a small fortune on his services, but that's not always the case.

"When a writer becomes defensive after I've shown him what's wrong with his script, I throw it at him and say, 'It's a *&^%! masterpiece,'" says McKee. If you are a writer, it's natural to defend your work, but doing so prevents you from learning how to make it better. The saying, "First thought, best thought" may be fine for distinctive songwriters like the pop star Charli XCX or the late Lou Reed, but for the rest of us, writing that's any good requires lots of rewriting, and being open to changes requires humility.

A writer I've known for many years sends me her work from time to time to ask my opinion. Nira has an unfortunate tendency to respond to my suggestions with justifications of her original choices. I don't go so far as tossing her work in her face with an expletive the way McKee does, but I have asked her more than once, "If you don't want to hear what I have to say, why are you running it by me in the first place?"

Perhaps Nira simply wants validation for her efforts, which are considerable. That's understandable. Who doesn't want to be told that their work is good, especially when they really apply themselves to it? But simply working hard isn't a guarantee of good results. The boss I had after leaving grad school used to repeat a saying of his mother's:

Never stop,
Never rest,
Until your good is better,
And your better is the best.

Humble people accept criticism graciously, because they know that constructive criticism can be of huge benefit in helping you step up your game. They also know that no matter how good you are, there's always room for improvement.

Nira has many wonderful qualities. She is warm, witty, and kind. Perhaps she is terribly insecure and masks that insecurity by appearing confident, even arrogant. But, whatever the reason, she isn't humble about her work. That lack of humility is holding her back from getting better at what she does.

Obstacles to Humility

Our Culture Doesn't Value Humility

I'm flipping through the channels on my TV. On CNBC it's *Shark Tank*. A young fellow in a bright red shirt is trying to persuade a panel of five wildly successful entrepreneurs to fund his start-up business, based on a product he believes will revolutionize Christmas celebrations: magnetic holiday lights. On HLN's *Dr. Drew on Call*, the host (a physician who is not technically on call during the program), four panelists, and selected viewers are debating whether a celebrity who has been charged with sexual assault in the court of public opinion is suffering from a medical condition or is "just a perverted...creep." The celebrity in question isn't on the program to defend himself against the accusations. I play a recording I made of last night's *Inside City Hall,* a political program on a local channel. Two Democratic and two Republican consultants are loudly arguing about nationwide protests against two recent court decisions. At several points, all four pundits speak at the same time, making the discussion unintelligible. (The overmodulated audio reminds me of what happened to my father's stereo when, at the age of six, I tested his microphone by yelling into it.) Each person in the discussion seems convinced he or she is right.

All of this arrogance stands in sharp contrast to the way Patrick Henry, a professor of religious studies at the college I attended, explained his view of faith. "I believe this with all my heart," he said. "But I may be wrong."

It's not surprising that chest-beating displays of bravado and certainty are valued in popular culture. With more and more forms of news and entertainment to choose from, each source has to be louder just to be heard above the din. Roger Chiang, who spent eight years as a television producer, notes that a common phrase among producers of reality television is "'This isn't loud enough.' They want chaos. They want fighting. Reality programming is reshaping the attitudes of our society." Where does humility fit into this landscape?

In defense of cable news debates, a humble pundit's soft-spoken demeanor does not necessarily make for good television. What prompts channel-surfers to watch a show and stay until the commercials (the real purpose of TV) is conflict between supremely confident people. But this reality supports my thesis: the values that make compelling television programs are antithetical to humility.

All is not lost, however. One of the most popular books of the past several years is Susan Cain's *Quiet.* It's not a book about humility exactly, but humility is often found in the kind of people

Cain describes. And humility can comfortably coexist with boldness. Warren Buffett is hardly a wallflower, but his humility comes across clearly in the interviews he gives, where he talks about his indebtedness to others and his commitment to repaying that debt.

Ours is a largely visual culture, in which far more people watch TV, go to the movies, and play video games than read books. To attract and retain viewers, producers and programmers are often compelled to keep ratcheting up the levels of conflict. In such a landscape, it's easy for representations of humility to be dismissed.

Many Successful People Have an Excess of Hubris, Not Humility

The title says it all: "Be a Jerk: The Worst Business Lesson from the Steve Jobs Biography." That's Tom McNichol's gloss on Walter Isaacson's biography of the creator and CEO of Apple. McNichol is troubled that one of the most successful people in the history of business was also "petulant, rude, spiteful, and controlling, a man who thought nothing of publicly humiliating employees, hogging the credit for work he hadn't done, throwing tantrums when he didn't get his way, or parking his Mercedes in handicapped spots." Jobs wasn't the only leader who could have benefited from a few basic lessons in civility. As McNichol notes, many Silicon Valley leaders believed Jobs's management style was necessary for achieving Apple's extraordinary success. Those leaders said as much to Robert Sutton, who wrote about them in his book *The No-A****** Rule: Building a Civilized Workplace and Surviving One That Isn't.*

But Charlie Ayers, the first head chef of Google, paints a very different picture. If Jobs saw that the table he'd reserved at Ayers's restaurant was occupied, he would wait. That's not the behavior one associates with someone as egotistical as Jobs was reported to be. If the restaurant was full when Jobs wanted a reservation, he would be content with a makeshift table next to the food coolers.

Granted, deferring to restaurant patrons with a bona fide reservation may not represent the pinnacle of humility, but it does show that some apparently domineering leaders have a humble side to them that their employees may not see. And imagine what the diners at the restaurant thought when they saw Jobs defer to them. "Inspiring" comes to mind.

Humility Is Misunderstood

Many people who concur with the definition of humility as "a modest or low view of one's own importance" argue that it is not a virtue. Jaana Woiceshyn, who teaches business ethics at the Haskayne School of Business at the University of Calgary and is the author of *How to Be Profitable and Moral,* is among them. "If we want to be happy and profitable, we must reject humility as a deterrent to achieving values and embrace pride," she states in a blog post titled "Why Humility Is Not a Virtue."

As Janice Piacente demonstrated, however, humility is properly understood not as a *low* view of oneself but rather as an *accurate* view of it. We're dependent on one another in a multitude of ways, and humble employees have the self-confidence to share the credit for their accomplishments. Humility isn't a deterrent to being proud. It's an essential component of it.

Even the icons of self-achievement — the mountain climber, the marathon runner, the CEO who began life in poverty — didn't succeed on their own. Humility is a corrective to the popular idea that you can achieve anything you want simply with determination and self-reliance. It reminds us that we're deeply connected to one another, and it is honorable to acknowledge this from time to time. "True humility is not thinking less of yourself," C. S. Lewis wrote. "It is thinking of yourself less."

Evaluating Humility

Humble people are, almost by definition, not disposed to call attention to their humility. Still, the discerning interviewer might use the following questions to discover the degree to which a job candidate or employee is truly humble or merely pretending to be.

Tell me about one of your proudest accomplishments. What was it, and how did you pull it off?

Janice Piacente came up with a novel way of getting attention for an important phone number. But she gave the credit for it to her team, because they were the ones who took her idea and made it a reality. It's not that she denied the role she played in the project's development, but simply that her humility dictated that she also acknowledge the contributions of others.

Astute interviewers listen carefully to how the candidate or employee answers this question. Does he focus primarily or exclusively on his own role in the achievement? Or does he, like Janice, talk about how others contributed to his success?

Humility and gratitude have the common thread of indebtedness to other people. In the interview scenario in chapter 6, Adriana revealed herself to be a grateful person, even though she used *grateful* only once in her remarks. Likewise, one needn't expect to hear an explicit reference to humility or being humble. It would be nice for the interviewee to say something like, "I'm humbled by this experience," but it's not necessary. And the person who does so isn't necessarily humble. He or she may simply be good at figuring out what the interviewer is looking for (or is using the guidelines from this book cynically).

Do you consider yourself a humble person?

Many of the HR directors I interviewed for this book told me that, with respect to such blunt questions as this one, "you'd be surprised what job candidates will tell you if you ask." It's hard to know from this question whether the interviewer considers humility to be a good thing or a bad thing.

In considering the response, interviewers should pay attention to the way the candidate talks about colleagues, direct reports, and supervisors from previous jobs. Do they talk, as Janice Piacente and Jon Taplin did, about helping others to succeed? Job interviewers and performance reviewers alike would serve their own organizations well by hiring and promoting servant-leaders like Janice and Jon.

Where have you seen examples of humility in action?

As I tried to think of how I would answer this question, nothing came to mind immediately. Humble people aren't easy to find in either popular culture or our own lives. After a few moments of reflection, however, I remembered Emily, a woman I knew when I worked at Lox, Stock and Bagels, a deli in San Antonio, Texas, during my senior year of high school. Emily's job was to keep the restaurant clean, which she did tirelessly and cheerfully. I can't recall her ever complaining about her job, even though it was far from glamorous and couldn't have paid very well either. When Keith, the owner of the restaurant, decided to return to Chicago, he chose Emily to replace him as the manager.

Emily didn't have extensive formal education or any job experience beyond janitorial work, so Keith would have to teach her how to run the business. It would have been easier for him to train a more experienced person, or to hire someone who already knew the job. But Emily was trustworthy, and she was good with people. The day after Keith offered her the job, she was the same humble person as a manager that she'd been as the janitor. I didn't get the feeling that she viewed herself as any more important in her new role than she did before. She treated me in exactly the same way: with kindness.

I haven't thought about Emily for a long time, and I'm glad that this last question prompted me to remember her. It's a good idea for interviewers to allow applicants some extra time of their own, if necessary, to think about the humble employees they've known. You never know what inspiring stories await.

When Janice Piacente told me about how she gives credit to her team, even though her ideas often begin with her, I was surprised. "Isn't leadership about generating ideas?" I asked her.

"Not to me," she replied. "Leadership is about bringing out the best in people."

SUMMARY

Humility is an accurate view of one's accomplishments and an awareness of how we depend on one another to get things done.

Humble employees inspire their coworkers, instill confidence in their supervisors, and move up quickly in their organizations.

Obstacles to humility include

- a culture that doesn't value humility
- successful people who are defined by hubris, not humility
- the mistaken notion that humility is a low or overly modest view of one's accomplishments

CHAPTER 8

LOYALTY

During the summer of 2014, a New England grocery store chain called Market Basket faced a crisis when its employees left in protest. All twenty thousand of them.

What were they upset about? Low wages? Not enough benefits? Terrible working conditions? No. As *CBS News Sunday Morning* reported, the employees quit because of their loyalty to the CEO, Arthur T. Demoulas. Arthur had just been given his own walking papers by the company's board of directors. The board didn't like Arthur's plan to give more of the company's revenue to employees and less to stockholders, so it fired him. His replacement was his own cousin, Arthur S. Demoulas.

Arthur T.'s commitment to serving the company's employees engendered profound loyalty. Even the store's customers got into the act: they boycotted the store, resulting in a loss of $1 million per day. With such overpowering support for the ousted CEO from employees and customers alike, the board had no choice but to allow Arthur T. to buy out his cousin, which he did to the tune of $1.5 billion. Christopher Mackin, a lecturer at the Rutgers School of Management and Labor Relations, said that such a large-scale demonstration against a company's leader is "unheard-of in corporate America. It's like 1776 — we get to pick who governs us."

Loyalty is the eighth quality of high-character employees. Hiring loyal people and creating a culture that sustains this loyalty provides a strong return on investment. According to the Great Place to Work Institute, businesses whose employees are deeply satisfied (a key indicator of loyalty) have lower turnover, better safety records, superior job applicants, and stronger marketplace performance than other businesses do. The businesses on *Fortune*'s list of the one hundred best companies to work for do almost twice as well as those in the Standard & Poor 500 and Russell 3000 indexes. When a business doesn't have to spend time, money, and human resources on replacing employees who leave, it can focus on serving its customers and generating revenue. In this chapter, we'll look at how loyal employees enrich the bottom line, advance an organization's mission, and prompt others to be their best.

What Is Loyalty?

Let's take a look at each of the characteristics that define loyal employees.

Loyal Employees Have Strong Emotional Ties to Their Employers

What's surprising about the Market Basket employees' protest is not its passion: employees hold spirited demonstrations all the time. It's what the passion is about: an intense devotion to the company's leader. Any workplace protest worth its salt is spirited, but how many protests are for rather than against the head of the organization?

Loyal employees are devoted to their employers, but that devotion has, and should have, limits. In *Grease*, when Olivia Newton John's Sandy sings "Hopelessly Devoted to You," she's not showing her loyalty to John Travolta's Danny: she's revealing her obsession with him. The Market Basket employees, on the other hand, were evincing a healthy, even admirable feeling about Arthur T. They were *hopefully* devoted to him. Arthur T. fought for his employees, and they fought for him in return. That's why their walkout was a sign of their high character.

But suppose that Arthur T.'s cousin had triumphed and remained the company's CEO. You wouldn't blame the employees for returning to work. In this economy, jobs aren't easy to come by, and a job under a less-than-desirable leader may be better than no job at all. Loyalty is devotion, but not blind devotion. Still, you wouldn't expect those returning employees to feel the same emotional ties to the company that they did under its previous leader.

Loyal Employees Represent Their Employers Honorably

A second way that high-character employees evince loyalty to their organizations is through their conduct outside work. One evening after I'd given a talk to long-term care providers at a hotel in Fargo, North Dakota, a woman who wasn't at the presentation got into the elevator with me while talking on her cell phone. In a ride that lasted all of thirty seconds, I heard her reveal information she said had been given to her confidentially. She laughed at how she would use this to benefit herself and how it would hurt her competition. She mentioned the names of her competitor and her own company. I don't know her name, but I'll refer to her as Gabriella, or Gabby for short.

Either Gabby was so immersed in her conversation that she didn't notice someone was a few inches away from her and could easily hear what she was saying, or she didn't care. What are the chances, after all, that a fellow passenger would be listening? Or that such a person might be a writer who would use the incident to make a point in a book about high-character employees?

Gabby may have a boatload of positive qualities, but loyalty to her company isn't one of them. Even if the sneaky maneuvering she described was going to result in a short-term financial gain for her employer, the fact that she was willing to publicly admit to stealing confidential information and mention the name of her employer in the same breath is, at the very least, lousy PR for her company. I for one would be reluctant to do business with them, since I know that at least one of their employees doesn't take privacy very seriously. Loose lips sink ships — and lose potential customers.

But shouldn't an employee be free to do as he or she pleases when not at work, especially in the evening? Does loyalty require an employee to be on guard at all times against doing or saying something that might embarrass the organization? Since I have the privilege of knowing a two-star general in the military, I thought I'd find out how the U.S. armed forces deal with the issue of responsible behavior after hours.

Retired Air Force Major General Sharon Dunbar, who is now the vice president of Human Resources for General Dynamics Mission Systems, told me that members of the military are expected to conduct themselves honorably at all times, whether or not they're in uniform. This means they have to be judicious in what they say and how they use social media (a topic we examined in the chapter on care) and other applications of technology. Were Gabby a military officer, her behavior would not only be viewed as dishonorable: it could be grounds for administrative punishment as conduct unbecoming of an officer or even prosecution if the information was considered to be of a sensitive or classified nature.

To be sure, the stakes are higher in the military than they are in many businesses. Gabby's secret-stealing may have cost her competitor a few clients, and her behavior cost her business the certain loss of one potential client (me). Were she doing the same thing as a member of America's armed forces, national security might be compromised and lives jeopardized.

But even in the business world, there could still be severe consequences if Gabby's actions came to light, because her company could face costly, embarrassing, and time-consuming legal challenges. In an age where anyone with a smartphone can easily make recordings that wind up on YouTube or the news, a supposedly private, off-hours conversation can destroy a career and tarnish a business's good name. Remember Kelly Blazek from the chapter on accountability? Her nastygram to one person appeared in major media outlets and caused a sensation in the worst way for her.

The take-home message is that a member of an organization is a de facto representative of that group on *and* off the job. Loyal, high-character employees recognize this, even if their employer does not or cannot explicitly state it. Gabby would do her company and her own reputation a favor simply by being aware of what's going on around her when she's talking on her phone in public.

Major General Dunbar, on the other hand, is one of the Good Ones. I've known her for over twenty years, and as a retired two-star general, she still honorably represents the U.S. military in all she does. The Gabbys of the world could learn a lot from her.

Loyal Employees Stand by Their Organizations... Up to a Point

Meet Tim Lockett. For thirty years, Tim worked at the Unilever soap-bar factory in Hammond, Indiana. Tim saw managers and employees come and go. He was the unofficial historian of the plant; if you needed to know something, anything, about the facility, Tim was the go-to guy.

And there's one more noteworthy aspect of Tim's tenure at Unilever. He never missed a day's work. He didn't take sick days or take personal days to attend ball games. No one in the history of the company, as far as its management can determine, ever had Tim's consecutive run of days on the job. Tim took loyalty as far as it could go and stood by his company to the end of his career.

Coworkers were in tears on Tim's last day of work. He was more than another employee on the assembly line; he was a confidant, a friend, a shoulder to cry on, a good listener. Coworker Doreen Soucy said Tim consoled employees who had lost parents or other family members, and she called him "inspiring." In the film *Tribute,* the hero, played by Jack Lemmon, is lauded as the kind of person "who can turn a hamburger into a banquet." That's how Tim Lockett's coworkers saw him. His loyalty made a difficult place to work more bearable, and his loyalty prompted others to follow suit.

Tim stood by his employer for an unusually long time, but loyalty to an organization need not mean making a lifetime commitment to it. It can simply be an alignment of one's behavior with the organization's values for however long one is employed. Also, I don't know if Tim Lockett ever showed up at work with a contagious illness, but if he did, that would have shown a misbegotten sense of loyalty. As we saw in the chapter on accountability, there's a moral difference between having a strong work ethic and being a workaholic. And recall the story of Doug, who did a training session with a contagious illness. He cared a lot about doing the job he was paid to do, but that commitment shouldn't have come at the expense of his clients' health — or his own.

Still, there are some jobs that *do* require going to the end of the line. One such job is commanding a ship. Lee Joon-seok was captain of the MV *Sewol*, a South Korean ferry carrying almost five hundred people, mostly high school students, when the vessel capsized on April 16, 2014. Passengers were instructed to stay in their cabins, but the captain ignored his own directive and was among the first to be rescued. Three hundred people died. In another maritime tragedy, Doloresco Schettino was captain of the Italian cruise ship *Costa Concordia*, which capsized and sank on January 13, 2012, killing thirty-two people on board. He too left his post to save himself. By abandoning their ships, the two captains violated the long-standing maritime tradition that "the captain goes down with the ship." It takes a man or woman of uncommon courage to be willing to observe this tradition, but that responsibility is inherent in the role of captain. Disloyalty on the job can kill.

Sometimes loyalty must give way to other concerns, such as protecting clients from harm and opposing illegal or unethical activities by an employer. James Nordgaard was right to alert the Securities and Exchange Commission (SEC) about improper transactions by his boss, Candace King Weir, the owner of the hedge fund Paradigm Capital. The SEC independently verified his allegations, but Nordgaard's employer demoted him from head trader to a low-level position just the same. Paradigm Capital may have considered Nordgaard a turncoat, but the SEC didn't see it that way and later fined the company $2.2 million for demoting him. High-character employees in fields other than marine transportation are not ethically required to go down with the ship. In situations like Nordgaard's, they shouldn't.

Loyal Entrepreneurs Stand by Their Investors

Suppose your business went belly-up, and filing for bankruptcy would wipe out a debt of tens of thousands of dollars. Would you proceed? Philip Davis was in this predicament when his popular soul-food restaurant in Cleveland, Phil the Fire, was forced to close down. "My partner, Kirk Wright, turned out to be a crook," Phil says. "I trusted the person who had introduced us, but I should have paid attention to some red flags." Phil compares Kirk to Bernie Madoff: "He ran a Ponzi scheme and swindled a lot of people, including me, out of their entire investments."

Several of Phil's friends and colleagues encouraged him to file for bankruptcy protection. Doing so would have enabled him to end his financial nightmare and start with a clean slate. But he chose not to. "A lot of people put their faith in me, and I would have destroyed that faith had I gone the bankruptcy route," he notes. "That choice would have meant I no longer had a legal obligation to repay the money they invested. But the way I look at it, my investors weren't investing in my business. They were investing in *me*. They were loyal to me, and there was no question that I was going to remain loyal to them."

It occurred to me that Phil's remaining loyal to his investors wasn't just good for its own sake. It could also help him attract future investors. After all, if you're looking for a person to oversee an investment, wouldn't you prefer to go with someone who will stand by you, no matter what? But Phil says that thought never entered his mind. "When I decided not to go bankrupt, I wasn't thinking about whether it would be a good PR move for me in the future. My only thoughts were with the relationships I had at the time. I intend to pay every single person back, no matter how long it takes me."

Phil is working hard to make that happen. In 2013, he came up with an idea for a shovel that pushes snow or leaves away and thereby minimizes back injuries. He created a prototype, which he called the Pushel, and it made its debut in the marketplace on QVC in early 2014. He did so well on the show that he was invited to return a month later. He's also striving to launch a national chain of eateries.

"All you really have is your integrity," Phil says. "For me, that means remaining loyal to the people who have put their faith in my business ventures."

Loyalty Is a Two-Way Street

"Loyalty is dead — killed off through shortening contracts, outsourcing, automation and multiple careers. Faced with what could be 50 years of work, who honestly wants to spend that much time with one company? Serial monogamy is the order of the day." That's the conclusion of Lynda Gratton, professor of management practice at the London Business School. When loyalty is viewed strictly as something that employers expect from employees, and many employees have trouble making ends meet even while working full time, it makes sense to scoff at the notion of a loyal employee today. Why should an employee pledge allegiance to a company that raises health insurance premiums each year, whose compensation doesn't keep up with cost-of-living increases, or which expects employees to be available around the clock?

As Phyllis Korkki points out in the *New York Times*, loyalty should be viewed more broadly. It doesn't apply only to how employees act toward employers; the reverse has to be considered, too. Our grandparents could stay at their companies for years because those companies stood by the people who worked for them. "Many were guaranteed longtime employment along with health care and a pension," Korkki writes. "Now many companies cannot or will not hold up their end of the bargain, so why should the employees hold up theirs? Given the opportunity, they'll take their skills and their portable 401(k)'s elsewhere." And even when employees are well compensated, that's no guarantee they'll stick around forever. Recall that Naomi, whom we met in the chapter on gratitude, had a well-paying job with benefits, but that wasn't enough to keep her there. She felt unappreciated. Now she is surrounded by colleagues who value what she does. Naomi has been with this employer for a long time and doesn't plan on leaving anytime soon.

Arthur T. Demoulas of Market Basket was so committed to the well-being of his twenty thousand employees that they fought successfully to have him reinstated after the company fired him. And Market Basket isn't the only company whose employees are fiercely loyal. Each year, *Fortune* magazine lists one hundred of the best companies in the U.S. to work for, based on a survey of over a quarter of a million employees. These companies aren't necessarily the largest ones or those with the deepest pockets. Along with Google (#1), Marriott International (#57), and PriceWaterhouseCoopers (#65), a recent list includes the staffing supplier CHG Healthcare Services (#16), the HR payroll company Ultimate Software (#20), and the accounting firm Plante Moran (#23). Even in these challenging economic times, there are plenty of businesses that are loyal to the people who work for them, and that loyalty is reciprocated.

Sean, the editor we met in chapter 6, argued that gratitude should flow in two directions, from managers to team members and back again. Loyalty should be bidirectional too, but on a larger scale, flowing between institutions and the people who work for them.

Is Disloyalty Beneficial?

Up until now, we've considered why loyalty is a hallmark of high-character employees and why it is in an organization's own

interest to hire and promote loyal people. But an alarming article by *Forbes* contributor Cameron King suggests that from an
employee's point of view, disloyalty is financially beneficial.
"Staying employed at the same company for over two years on
average is going to make you earn less over your lifetime by about
50% or more," King writes, and he provides substantial evidence
to support this claim.

The average raise that an employee gets is 1 percent of his or
her salary, once the cost of inflation is figured in. But employees
get a salary increase between 10 percent and 20 percent when they
change jobs. King gives an example of what this means over a
ten-year period: "Jessica Derkis started her career earning $8 per
hour ($16,640 annual salary) as the YMCA's marketing manager.
Over 10 years, she's changed employers five times to ultimately
earn $72,000 per year at her most recent marketing position. This
is approximately a 330% increase over a 10-year career. Derkis's
most recent transition resulted in a 50% increase to her salary."

King doesn't mention what organizations Derkis has worked
for other than the Y. If they are for-profit companies, they may
have been able to afford to pay Derkis more for similar work.
But it's also possible that Derkis could have negotiated a higher
salary at the Y before she left. "Businesses often come up with
the money to match or exceed the offer an employee gets from a
rival," a senior financial manager told me in response to this article. "If they're able to find the resources to keep someone ready
to leave, why can't they pay that employee adequately to begin
with?"

It's tempting to conclude that an employee has to choose
between the financial benefits of disloyalty and the intangible benefits — long-term, meaningful relationships with team members
and clients, for example — of loyalty. If the bottom line of one's
career is the bottom line, then disloyalty makes financial sense.

"As an individual, you're a CEO of one, and you have a duty to maximize your profits," King concludes.

But this dichotomy doesn't have to exist in the first place. King's article should be a wake-up call to employers who want to keep high-character people on board: don't wait until the Good Ones threaten to leave to pay them well. This should also prompt employees who are tempted to leave their current positions to negotiate for higher raises so that they enjoy the benefits of sticking around. "You can't win if you don't play" should be the motto for upwardly mobile employees as well as state lotteries.

Evaluating Loyalty

In the previous chapter, I suggested that humility is difficult to evaluate, because people who are humble tend not to call attention to their accomplishments. Loyalty must be the easiest, right? All you have to do is see how long a job candidate has stayed in previous jobs, or find out when a current employee seeking a raise or promotion started to work at the organization.

But length of employment doesn't necessarily correlate to loyalty. The true measure of loyalty is the employee's attitude toward the company, other employees, clients, and his or her personal relationships, as well as how that attitude is manifested. The following questions may help an interviewer or reviewer get a better sense of this.

How have you responded at a previous job when a better opportunity with another employer came along?

Even for someone who has just begun his or her career, loyalty doesn't necessarily mean turning down a job offer. Character is revealed by *how* one responds to the offer, not whether or not one accepts it.

Suppose a job candidate — let's call her Emma — works for

Nadir Pitchforks, which hasn't treated her well. She learns of a similar position that has opened at Acme Halos. Emma is a loyal person and, all things being equal, would rather not have to switch jobs, but it would be self-defeating to stay with the pitchfork people. As Phyllis Korkki points out, employees can't be expected to stick around if their companies aren't doing right by them. How can Emma show the halo folks that she really is loyal? And how can she avoid bad-mouthing Nadir, which would be unprofessional even if her criticism is justified?

It would be smart for Emma to focus on why Acme's offer is irresistible, not on why she wants to leave Nadir. She might also talk about how she has demonstrated loyalty to other employers, perhaps even at Nadir Pitchforks. (She may have, for example, worked diligently there for quite awhile before problems arose.) If Emma doesn't have much work experience, she could talk about other life choices that demonstrate loyalty.

Has a valued employee who reported to you ever left the company because of a better opportunity elsewhere? If so, how did you respond to the employee? If not, how would you respond?

I began my career as a professor at the West Virginia University Health Sciences Center. Within a year of my appointment, a prestigious think tank invited me for an interview. It was a tremendous honor, but I worried about being disloyal to my employer and told one of my senior colleagues, David, about my concerns. I'll never forget how he responded.

"This would be a great opportunity," David said as he drove me to the airport in Morgantown. "We want the best for you." That alleviated my anxiety enormously, because had I been offered the job, I could have accepted it knowing that I wasn't letting the university down. Although I wasn't offered the position, the whole experience was worth it just to have experienced

David's graciousness. He led by example, and I hope to respond the same way to a younger colleague if the situation ever arises.

No employer wants a valuable employee to leave, but sometimes an opportunity comes along that is too good to pass up. A job applicant who answers this question along the lines of David's response is someone who recognizes that loyalty doesn't have to mean staying with one employer for years. Such a person is one of the Good Ones.

What were some of the things you liked most about your previous (or current) job?

A peculiar aspect of the working life is that during the week we spend more time with our coworkers than we do with our own families. Feeling connected to colleagues, having a good time with them during breaks and at meals, and getting advice from people who know us well are three of the biggest sources of enjoyment in our careers. "Very few of us, and none of the people I deal with, work for just a paycheck," says Alan Murray, editor of *Fortune* magazine. "We need the paycheck, we want the paycheck, we'll negotiate for the paycheck, but we also work for other types of satisfaction."

Managers should care about whether their employees are satisfied for several reasons. First, satisfied employees tend to be loyal employees. They stick around. Second, satisfied employees are more likely to be productive and enjoy good relationships with customers, which promotes repeat business. John Mackey, the founder of Whole Foods, says that when the people who work at the company "are happy and enjoy their work, they give better service to the customers. And then if customers are happy, they continue to shop at the store, they market through word of mouth, and the business flourishes. It prospers."

How would a job candidate who values loyalty answer this

question? Talking about a strong relationship with a previous boss is crucial. As the Market Basket story suggests, caring managers engender fiercely loyal employees. One would also expect to hear the candidate discuss close ties with colleagues. Robert Levering, a creator of *Fortune*'s "100 Best Companies to Work For," says that employees at those top companies said they felt as though they were part of a team or even a family. That may be why Whole Foods, one of *Fortune*'s top companies, refers to the people who work there as "team members."

It's worth paying special attention to the nonverbal signals in a candidate's response to this question. It's hard to fake joy. When someone talks about an experience working in a team- or family-like environment, for a boss who truly cares about the employees, the positive feelings that go along with the words are palpable. Watch the *CBS News Sunday Morning* report about Market Basket, and look at the faces of employees when they get their boss back. That's the look of true satisfaction — and loyalty.

SUMMARY

Loyal employees

- have strong emotional ties to their employers
- represent their employers honorably
- stand by their employers

Loyalty means aligning one's behavior with the organization's values for however long one is employed.

Loyalty is a two-way street: organizations that are loyal to their employees are more likely to have employees who are loyal to them.

CHAPTER 9

PATIENCE

I once saw a photograph of a dandelion plant. On its own, that image wouldn't be anything special: dandelions are everywhere. But these dandelions were nestled atop a small mound of asphalt. Somehow they had managed to push through this seemingly impermeable barrier and reach their goal: bathing in sunlight and fresh air. If there is a better illustration of patience than this photograph, I've yet to see it.

High-character employees are like these dandelions: they keep pushing on with their mission until they prevail. They don't allow themselves to be diverted from their path by external forces, and their persistence pays off. You may not think dandelions are beautiful, but I think you'll agree that from their perspective, their struggle was a matter of life and death — and they lived. Isn't that the greatest beauty of all?

The Four Elements of Patience

Acceptance

God grant me the serenity to accept the things I cannot change; the courage to change the things I can; and the wisdom to know the difference.

—Attributed to Reinhold Niebuhr

In 2010, when Bono, the lead singer of U2, developed a herniated disc and needed to have emergency back surgery, he was faced with more than an unpleasant health problem. He and the band were in the middle of a two-year worldwide tour. "We had to cancel a million tickets," Bono said with great dismay. At stake were the millions of dollars the band and its employees would lose, as well as the hopes of a million fans.

Paul McGuinness, the band's manager, called their concert promoter, Arthur Fogel, to relay the bad news. "I called Arthur at 4 in the morning, his time, in L.A.," Paul said. "I was in Ireland, and I've never done that before, and so he knew that it must be something serious, [and it] couldn't have been worse in terms of the schedule."

Arthur Fogel is no ordinary concert promoter. He has managed four of the top five highest-grossing musical tours in history, and his client list includes some of the most popular groups in the entertainment world, such as Rush, Madonna, Lady Gaga, the Police, and the Rolling Stones. Paul therefore had good reason to believe that Arthur would not take the news well. But that's not what happened.

"I walk up into his office and just look at him," said Joey Scoleri, one of Arthur's direct reports. "It was just announced that morning that the shows were being postponed, [and I expect that] he's gonna be stressed and white-knuckling. And he just looks at me and he goes, 'Just another day at the office — just a busier one.'" The tour was delayed a year at a potential cost of $100 million in ticket sales and what McGuinness called "the biggest insurance claim of all time, in our business anyway."

"When Arthur came into the room," Bono says of his hospital stay, "he was just completely calm, completely serene.... He's George Clooney in *ER*: good looking guy, comes in when the room's about to explode, and he calms the patient's nerves and performs open-heart surgery with a Swiss army knife." Arthur Fogel accepted a reality he could not change, stood by his client, kept the public informed throughout, maintained their trust, and ultimately lost very few ticket sales. *That's* the power of acceptance.

I'm writing this part of the book on a plane. I spent far too much money to get internet access during the flight so I could do research for this book, check some facts, and see how many "likes" my latest Facebook post has gotten. The flight is almost over now, and for most of it, I couldn't get a good connection. After having a few web pages freeze and remain frozen, the smart thing for me to do would have been to recognize that the service wasn't working well, give up on it, and do something more productive like actually write, or even take a nap.

But each time I got locked out, the more stubborn I became in believing that with enough effort I could gain access to the all-important World Wide Web — and the angrier I got, too. I mentally drafted the clever, hostile letter I'd write to the company demanding a full refund for their shoddy internet service. The more heated I became, the more difficult it was to do the work I'd wanted the instant access for in the first place.

Had I accepted the situation, as Arthur Fogel probably would have, I'd have used my time more wisely (and wouldn't have gotten so angry, either). There are some things we can change, and some things we can't. To be patient is to know the difference and to act (or not act) on it. People like Arthur understand how the world works, and they don't try to impose their will onto it. It's a winning attitude, and that's why Arthur Fogel is one of the Good Ones.

Flexibility

Cara Lemieux is a former network news producer and digital communications strategist whose clients include the *Shriver Report*, a nonprofit media initiative created by Maria Shriver. She also created the blog *Me & Ducky* as a sounding board for single mothers like her. "Patience is not my strong suit," Cara says, "but I've learned the necessity of patience from being a single mom — because not everything I want done can be done instantly anymore." An essential element of patience for Cara is flexibility.

"My daughter's needs are constantly changing, and I have to adapt or I can't be a good mom," she told me. "Infants get twelve to fifteen illnesses a year, so when my daughter was a baby, I needed to be able to care for her when she was sick. Now that she is in pre-kindergarten, I may need to leave work early to go to a play or a school picnic. Flexibility is strength. What's going to hold up better when something is pressing against it — a glass window or a cotton sheet? You have to adapt."

Becoming more flexible in her personal life has helped Cara become more flexible in her professional role. This sometimes means taking over for colleagues who have to tend to their own personal lives.

Persistence

Seven years after she graduated from college, Jo felt like a failure. Her marriage had collapsed, she didn't have a job, and she had a child who was dependent on her for survival. Her mother had died, and Jo had been diagnosed with clinical depression. She was so despondent that she considered taking her own life.

But Jo had a dream: she wanted to write a novel. In fact, she had developed an extensive blueprint for a series of novels about a boy with magical skills, and she believed that her sprawling story, rich with imagined details, would be compelling. Jo wrote the first novel and found a literary agent to represent her. That agent loved the book, but it took him a year to find a publisher who wanted to run with it.

You know Jo better as J. K. Rowling, and the seven books she wrote about a boy wizard named Harry Potter developed a worldwide following unmatched to this day. Rowling is the richest author in the world; one source estimates her personal fortune to be close to a billion dollars. She is a generous philanthropist through her charitable trust, whose main interests are finding a treatment for multiple sclerosis (the cause of her mother's death) and alleviating social deprivation, especially for women and children. As someone who never gave up on her dream, she is an inspiration to all of us.

This isn't to say that Rowling never felt doubtful about achieving her goal. She sometimes felt discouraged but pressed on. Rowling experienced a lot of the negative emotions you'd expect on her journey — self-doubt, fear of failure — but she didn't let them derail her. In fact, her 2008 commencement address at Harvard University was called "The Fringe Benefits of Failure, and the Importance of Imagination."

In the *Journal of Finance*, Steven N. Kaplan, Mark M. Klebanov, and Morten Sorensen reported that in their study of over three hundred CEOs of financial investment firms, the most successful ones were also the most persistent. "Persistent leaders don't give up," Kaplan writes. "They stick with assignments until they are done."

Positive reinforcement helps us be persistent. If you decide to begin an exercise program, you may get winded after a few minutes of jogging on the first few days, but after a while you find you can go for twenty, then thirty, then forty-five minutes without getting tired. It's that sense of progress that motivates you to keep going.

But, as in Rowling's case, sometimes you don't see positive results — or any results — for a long time. What kept Rowling on track was her belief in herself and in the value of what she was doing. As Paulo Coelho wrote in his novel *Brida*, "None of us knows what might happen even the next minute, yet still we go forward. Because we trust. Because we have Faith."

Rowling's struggle isn't limited to writers. "Here in Memphis, every successful employee I know can relate to what Ms. Rowling went through," says Jeremy C. Park, president of the Lipscomb Pitts Breakfast Club, whose 150 events each year bring together business and community leaders for philanthropic work in the Mid-South. "Whatever their line of work happens to be — delivering goods and services, teaching in a classroom, shaping public policies, or serving the neediest in our neighborhoods — those who flourish know that taking small steps on a regular basis, no matter what, is the surest way to fulfill the missions of their organizations and also enrich their own lives. Persistence is power."

J. K. Rowling's story is the perfect illustration of persistence: no matter how many obstacles she encountered — and there were many — she never gave up. She is one of the Good Ones because her patience resulted in one of the defining stories in popular culture that continues to enthrall children and adults. High-character employees who practice patience are like Jo: they know that waiting can be immensely rewarding.

Delaying Gratification

My wife Kristen and I have opposite approaches to an essential element of the good life: eating cake. I proceed immediately to the part with most of the icing on it, because I want the best part now. Why wait? Kris, on the other hand, insists on saving the best bite for last. She wants to end the experience on the highest note.

There's no right or wrong way to eat a piece of cake. But there is something to be said for delayed gratification. In research that came to be known as the Stanford Marshmallow Experiment, Stanford psychology professor Walter Mischel and colleagues offered children the opportunity to have a marshmallow now — or, if they were willing to wait, two marshmallows fifteen minutes later. Follow-up studies revealed that the children who had been willing to wait for the treats were more successful than the children who wanted fulfillment immediately. The delayed-gratification group overall had higher SAT scores, a lower body mass index, longer and healthier relationships, and greater success in other areas of professional and personal achievement. In other words, patience pays off.

A subsequent study at the University of Rochester by the cognitive science graduate student Celeste Kidd and her team, as well as early work by Mischel himself, indicates that a factor other than willpower may play a role in a person's ability to delay gratification: trust. Children who believed that the researcher was telling the truth were more likely to choose two treats later; children who had been conditioned to see the researcher as untrustworthy chose to have one treat now. (Can you blame them?) Kidd's work suggests that it takes more than willpower to be a patient person. High-character employees are willing to delay immediate gratification because they trust that something better is within reach, in time.

High-character employees are adept at restraining the impulses we all have for immediate satisfaction. They recognize that sometimes our impulses have to be subordinated to a higher good. Before her success, J. K. Rowling said she "felt life was a train wreck.... I was in this place that was very alien and cold, and quite grim," but she patiently worked toward her goal of telling the story of Harry Potter. Patient employees, the organizations they work for, and the people they serve are all beneficiaries of patience. Maybe Kristen really does have a better approach to eating cake. I need to remind myself of something I was told on my wedding day: "Your wife is always right!"

Learning Patience the Hard Way

Ed Krow was furious. He was a manager in the HR department of a Fortune 100 shipping company, and his supervisor had just announced a promotion. "I knew I was in the running for it, but another guy in the department, Willis, got it. And he was a friend of mine. But I felt I deserved it. I was not only disappointed — I was angry."

Ed learned about the decision through the grapevine and began expressing his anger to his colleagues before Ed's supervisor made the official announcement. Ed's bad-mouthing eventually made its way back to Willis. "My boss called me into his office and told me he didn't like my reaction. He was right. I apologized to him and then to Willis for how I handled the news. Willis could have easily said, 'What a jerk,' but to his credit, he was more of a man than I was. He put his arm around me and said, 'I accept your apology. Let's move on.'"

Apologizing for losing his temper "wasn't only the right thing to do," Ed says. "It was the smart thing to do. Here was a guy who was now in a position that could help me in the future. You know that old adage about not burning your bridges? Well, I had lit the match! In retrospect, I see that Willis *was* the person who should have gotten the promotion. He was the better person for the job than I at the time."

Their friendship recovered. "Both of us eventually left the company, and we kept in touch. He took over a school bus company, I started an HR consulting business — and now he's one of my clients! I'm lucky that things turned out the way they did, because it could have derailed my career. I learned a valuable lesson: it's OK to be disappointed, but to undermine a decision is not an appropriate reaction."

Anger is the most troubling emotion in the workplace because of the damage it can cause. There are several ways of dealing with anger at work. You can express it the way that Ed did and then have to backpedal and make amends. Or you can acknowledge the hurt feelings but restrain the impulse to act on them. Employees who are patient do the latter.

Ed grew from his experience of indiscreetly expressing anger. He remembers how close he came to damaging a valuable relationship and tarnishing his career by giving way to anger and disappointment. Ed no longer lets those emotions get the better of him. As a result, he has become better at accepting situations that he cannot change. "I don't know if you can ever master the art of the relationship," he says, "but I've gotten better at being aware of what I'm thinking when things aren't going my way. Then I ask myself, 'Is what I'm about to say to someone going to help build a relationship with that person, or is it going to put a brick in the wall between us?' If my thought is hurtful, I just keep it to myself. And this way of thinking has done wonders for me." Having such self-awareness and self-restraint is exactly what it means to be patient. And that's why Ed Krow is one of the Good Ones.

How Patient Employees Benefit Their Organizations

"The angrier the other person gets, the cooler you should become." That was my dad's advice to me when I joined the workforce. Although I recognized its wisdom, I found it difficult to put into practice. When I'm around people who are angry, frazzled, or anxious, I'm affected by their feelings. As Mitchell Kusy and Elizabeth Holloway describe in their book *Toxic Workplace!*, employees with difficult personalities can create an environment that impedes productivity, damages morale, and makes coming to work an emotionally draining experience.

Patient employees, on the other hand, can have a calming effect on their colleagues. Andi Sciacca, director of the Center for Excellence in Teaching and Learning at the Culinary Institute of America in Hyde Park, New York, told me about an employee named Craig B. Laub, whose patience has a profound impact on the faculty and staff there. Craig works in the institute's audiovisual department, which, along with IT, must be one of the most stressful jobs around. "People are constantly making demands of Craig," Andi says, "but he focuses on solutions and doesn't let the craziness get to him." Remaining calm amid the chaos has a positive effect on others. "People see how patient he is, and they want to be more like him. His title is AV technician, but he's more like Gandalf because of his incredible ability to help."

In the introduction, I drew on the work of Aristotle to suggest that each trait associated with high-character employees is a mean between two extremes. Craig Laub's calmness, an aspect of patience, lies somewhere between agitation and lethargy. He is neither tightly wound nor lazy, but he can switch gears when the situation calls for it.

One day Andi was accompanying Temple Grandin, who was about to speak on the campus, and Andi had to change the venue at the last minute. "I shot Craig an email at 7 in the morning and asked him if there was any way to make it work. He responded right away, said he'd be right on it, and got the job done. He didn't have to be at work then, and he could easily have gotten someone else to take care of the problem, but he did it cheerfully." When Andi says that Craig "makes it possible for other people to shine," I'm reminded of how Janice Piacente, whom we met at the beginning of the chapter on humility, says that the job of a leader is to "bring out the best in other people."

Craig Laub's patience is infectious. "I can be having the worst possible day, one of those days when nothing is going right and you question why you even bothered coming to work," Andi explains, "but when I see Craig, I feel inspired. I'm in the hospitality industry, and we're supposed to be focused on service, but it's easy to forget that goal when you have mounting deadlines."

Craig's patience allows him to serve the organization well and to inspire the people he works with, and for these reasons he is one of the Good Ones. And Andi's humility in recognizing her own limitations and her readiness to express gratitude to people like Craig makes her one of the Good Ones too.

How Impatient Employees Hurt Organizations

Eileen Gray has served as an HR manager for over thirty years and is president of the Atlanta chapter of the National Association of African Americans in Human Resources. At the beginning of her career, she worked for an organization whose HR director, Carrie, had anger-management problems.

Carrie's office was next to Eileen's. Early in Eileen's employment at the organization, she overheard Carrie yelling at an employee. "I'll never forget it," Eileen told me. "Even though this was three decades ago, I remember well. One of her direct reports had a doctorate and worked in training and development, and Carrie was angry with something the direct report had done." What bothered Eileen wasn't just the intensity of Carrie's anger; it was the fact that Carrie was making personal attacks. "Carrie was saying things like, 'How were you smart enough to get a PhD?' You can get angry with someone else's decision or an action that they took, but to berate the person and question their credibility is out of bounds. That's not a fair play. If we were playing a sport, I'd cry 'foul.'"

This wasn't the first time that Eileen had seen Carrie erupt in anger because of her impatience; it was a pattern of behavior that had a chilling effect on the people who worked with and for Carrie. "It made me so guarded in my interactions with Carrie, because I didn't want her to get angry with me and question my education and qualifications to be there," Eileen said.

Why didn't Eileen tell Carrie about her concerns? "It was early in my career, and I was anxious to work there. I knew Carrie had a short fuse, so something in me shut down. I didn't want to bring her any news that might upset her."

What makes Eileen's story especially disturbing is that the angry employee was the head of the human resources department — the place where employees go to report other employees who are acting inappropriately. If the head of that department is a problematic employee herself, how can employees feel safe talking about their troubles? Carrie reported to the president of the company, and both had been in those positions for a long time. If a newcomer like Eileen had gone directly to him, it's easy to imagine that the president would have sided with Carrie, which might have jeopardized Eileen's standing in the company and made her relationship with Carrie even more tenuous.

"Did you see any sign of Carrie's anger during your job interview?" I asked Eileen.

"Not at all. In fact, she was charming and delightful," Eileen replied. "Had I known what she was really like, I don't think I would have taken the job." She couldn't take Carrie's impatient leadership style and eventually left the company.

Of course, impatience does not necessarily result in anger and is not necessarily a bad thing. It can prompt us to take action when we need to. Recall David Dawit Searles's story from the beginning of the chapter on fairness. David has no patience with people who make inappropriate remarks in the workplace, which led him to call out a United States senator for doing just that. But Eileen Gray's boss was impatient in the wrong way, and that impatience boiled over into white-hot rage. In their book *Anger Kills*, Redford Williams and Virginia Williams present evidence that angry people are at increased risk of life-threatening illnesses. Eileen's story illustrates that anger also poisons relationships and the workplace itself.

Obstacles to Patience

If patience is such a valuable quality for employees to have, why is it so elusive? Three things may get in the way of developing or maintaining this trait.

The Demand for Fast, Quantifiable Results

When we were young, our years were divided into fall (school), spring (school), and summer (play). As we grew older, summer play gave way to summer jobs, but life was still one long stretch of schoolwork, punctuated by a few months of a full-time job.

Corporate life slashes the year into four parts. Business is driven by quarterly results that must please a board of directors, and the pursuit of those results is the enemy of patience. Even in other sectors of the economy, where life isn't ruled by quarters, the need to produce measurable results sooner rather than later makes patience a vice, not a virtue.

The mad dash for quick results isn't just maddening; it's harmful to an organization's long-term interests. That's the conclusion of Robert C. Prozen's *Harvard Business Review* blog post, "Can We Break the Tyranny of Quarterly Results?" "Short-term myopia directly impacts a firm's ability to innovate," Prozen argues, citing a survey by the National Bureau of Economic Research in which the vast majority of senior financial executives admitted they were willing to stop spending on research and development and delay investments that had long-term return potential in order to meet quarterly projections. Decisions like this create a vicious cycle of cutting corners and jeopardizing future benefits for the sake of immediate results.

Despite a business culture that seems to clamor for rapid results, pushing hard for them isn't always beneficial: When Ron Johnson left Apple to run J. C. Penney, his radical overhaul of the company's stores and image went over like a lead zeppelin, and he was quickly shown the door. A similar fate befell Meg Whitman in her attempt to turn Hewlett-Packard around. As Michael Schrage points out in another HBR blog post, "Are You Driving Too Much Change, Too Fast?," companies like IBM and Procter & Gamble have succeeded through a slow-but-steady leadership approach.

A company is more likely to attract and keep patient employees when its leader values patience and practices it consistently.

The Rewards of Impatience

Before I started graduate school, I spent half a year putting together the first statewide conference on what were then called hospital ethics committees. My office was in a hospital administration department, and one of the women who worked there was responsible for paying me through a grant I'd obtained. But it took a long time for the hospital to cut my first paycheck. I was patient for as long as I could manage, but after weeks of getting nowhere, I slammed my fist against the door of the woman's office and yelled, "I expect to be paid tomorrow!" And I was.

Thirty years after this shameful episode, it makes me blanch to recall it. I'm not sure if my outburst is what got the ball rolling or if it was just a coincidence, but I will admit that it made me feel powerful to display such anger and to get quick results.

Anger is an expression of impatience, but we couldn't banish anger or other negative thoughts, even if we wanted to. In their article "Emotional Agility," Susan David and Christina Congleton state, "Effective leaders don't buy into *or* try to suppress their inner experiences. Instead they approach them in a mindful, values-driven, and productive way." When we become angry, they recommend becoming aware of the anger, to take a "helicopter view" of ourselves. By distancing ourselves in this way, we can calm down and act according to our values. Had I been mature enough thirty years ago to do this, I would have seen that reacting angrily to the administrator might secure a short-term goal but risked damaging a long-term one: maintaining a good relationship with a colleague. That relationship didn't suffer any lasting injuries, but I was lucky. Impatience may get results, but at what cost?

The Role of Technology

Back in the old days, say in the 1990s, businesses would send memos on paper to alert the staff of upcoming committee meetings, changes in company protocol, and the like. The boss dictated the memo, a secretary typed it, someone else photocopied it, and a fourth person distributed the photocopies. This process took a minimum of a few hours, and more often a day or two. The boss *had* to be patient; there was no other choice. Today, we get upset if someone doesn't reply to our emails within minutes.

Delaying gratification is the fourth element of patience, so it makes sense to ask how technology affects our ability to do it. It's easy to blame our devices for this problem. But even if technology has made rapid communication possible in corporate life, it doesn't follow that technology *causes* us to be impatient. There is such a thing as free will, and as tempting as it is to expect things to happen when we want them to, we can choose either to get upset when our expectations are dashed or to accept the reality that some things are out of our control and practice patience.

When David Jenkins of the pop band Pablo Cruise sang, "And all at once you're ready to hang it up / 'Cause things didn't turn out the way you planned," he was referring to a rocky romance, but he may as well have been talking about our increasing impatience about getting things done at work. We can blame technology for our problems, but as the comic-strip character Pogo said, "We have met the enemy, and he is us." Put another way: Are we controlling technology, or are we allowing technology to control us?

Evaluating Patience

Carrie, Eileen Gray's first boss, lacked patience and lashed out in anger whenever things didn't go her way. Arthur Fogel was dealt an enormous setback as a concert promoter when U2's Bono needed emergency back surgery in the middle of a tour, but Arthur rose to the challenge graciously and patiently. How can an employer determine whether a job candidate is more like Carrie or more like Arthur? Asking the candidate, "Do you consider yourself to be a patient person?" won't work, because impatient people tend to attribute their outbursts to external factors; they may honestly believe that they are the epitome of patience.

The following questions may help employees get a better sense of a job candidate's capacity for patience.

Tell me about a time when something at work deeply frustrated you, but you kept calm and dealt with the problem.

The angel is in the details here, and the details are the subject's nonverbal cues. Pathological liars aside, it would be difficult for a job candidate to tell a convincing story about how he or she patiently handled a challenge at work if it weren't true. When I'm around an impatient person, I feel ill at ease. On the flip side, as Bono notes, a calm person has a calming presence. The smart interviewer, therefore, pays attention to how he or she feels when the candidate is telling the story. (Of course, the interviewer should check in with him- or herself to be sure that any feelings of unease aren't the result of unconscious bias, as I discuss in the introduction.)

When have you lost your cool at work, and what happened as a result?

Even Arthur Fogel, I'm sure, has his bad days. Maybe Mahatma Gandhi did too (though it's hard to imagine him reaming someone out for a mistake). Unless this is the first job the candidate has ever applied for, "I've never lost my cool" is not a realistic response.

Still, a job candidate might worry that admitting to losing his temper might be a strike against him. The interviewer might reassure him, "Don't worry. You won't get any points deducted for admitting you've gotten angry at work. We all have." The interviewer might even give an example from his or her own experience that will encourage the candidate to tell his own story.

The interviewer should look for a sense of regret or remorse as the story is being told. I'm ashamed of myself for the way I treated that hospital administrator thirty years ago, and if I told you the story in person, I'd hope you'd feel my regret. The point of asking this question is to learn not only what the candidate did in the circumstances but also how it affected him or her. What did the candidate learn from the incident? Did she apologize or change her behavior afterward? Did he become a better employee — and a better person?

After Ed Krow bad-mouthed his colleague Willis, Ed came to see how undignified his behavior was and apologized to Willis. What impressed me about Ed's story was his admission that in hindsight Willis was the better man for the job. Ed learned a powerful lesson in patience and humility from the experience, and he was rewarded years later by gaining Willis as a client.

Tell me about a project you worked on that took longer to complete than you had anticipated. What was the project, what got in the way, and how did you deal with those obstacles?

This question touches on all four elements of patience: flexibility, acceptance, delayed gratification, and persistence.

It's not necessary to spend years on a project, as J. K. Rowling did, to demonstrate patience. If a candidate had good reason to believe that a project was going to take a couple of weeks but turned out to require several months, seeing it through to the end could demonstrate an admirable degree of patience. A lot of business deals fall into this category.

Job candidates who refer to flexibility as a critical component of their success are on the right track. Again, though, one wants to hear exactly what that flexibility amounted to. Did it involve shifting the work-life balance when family issues arose, as Cara did, or was some other factor involved? Candidates who tell a story like the ones in this chapter and do so credibly are likely to be patient people who will therefore be a credit to the institution.

It's useful to include a discussion about patience in an employee's performance review. An assessment of this quality will probably not be in the employee's record, so the above questions offer a way of finding out the degree to which patience has played a role in the employee's success.

These questions may also reveal the candidate's humility. Perhaps he or she was partly to blame for the project's taking longer than expected. Candidates who include their own mistakes among the obstacles they faced are to be commended for being appropriately humble.

SUMMARY

To be patient is to be flexible, accepting, willing to delay gratification, and persistent.

Obstacles to patience include the results-driven nature of corporate life, the fact that impatience is often rewarded, and technology that fuels the desire for instant gratification.

CHAPTER 10

PRESENCE

On October 7, 2011, Ann Zuccardy was getting into a bathtub when she fell and hit her head against the tile wall. Afterward she felt dizzy and slurred her words a little bit, but didn't think anything of it until she went to work and things got worse. "I didn't do anything at first, because, hey, I've given birth at home, in my living room, with no drugs — I can handle this!" she said. But in fact she couldn't handle it, so she went to her physician, who sent her to the hospital. Ann was diagnosed with a near-fatal brain trauma called a coup-contrecoup injury.

Ann's life turned upside down. An intellectually gifted woman, Ann had prided herself on her ability to blaze through books quickly and retain everything she read. Now it was a struggle to get through a single page of text. Crossing the street and going down stairs became monumentally difficult. She lost her short-term memory, finding it impossible to recall what day of the week it was. As she puts it in her TED talk, "I became depressed, not because of what I couldn't do anymore, but because I was no longer smart."

But Ann's accident prompted her to develop presence, the tenth and final crucial quality of high-character employees. She focuses on the tasks before her, one at a time. She is aware of distractions and upsetting emotions that can get her off course, but she doesn't let them derail her. Ann's remarkable comeback from trauma is a great illustration of what presence is and why it is in an organization's best interests to hire people who exhibit it.

Must Be Present to Win

Don't try to do two things at once and expect to do justice to both.
— Opening title card in Buster Keaton's film *Sherlock, Jr.* (1924)

What does it mean for an employee to be present? Simply showing up? That's not enough. If Herb makes a lot of personal calls instead of doing his job, he is at work only in the most superficial sense.

What about Jane, who multitasks by keeping social media tabs open on her computer or mobile device? Jane seems to be more present than Herb; at least she's doing some work. The problem is that our brains aren't built to multitask. When we jump from one electronic activity to another and back to the first one, we're actually doing each task less well than we would if our attention were given over completely to it. Jane's multitasking thus compromises her ability to be fully present in both her work and her social media.

Multitasking at one's desk is merely inefficient. Doing it behind the wheel is potentially fatal. Courtney Sanford was in a good mood on the morning of April 24, 2014, so she let her friends know about it by posting a note on her Facebook page. She was at the wheel of her car when she sent the message. A moment later her car crossed the median and slammed into a truck, and she died. Just before being killed, she had posted: "The happy song makes me HAPPY!"

Courtney's tragic story is becoming more common. According to the Centers for Disease Control and Prevention, "Each day in the United States, more than 9 people are killed and more than 1,153 people are injured in crashes that are reported to involve a distracted driver." Using a cell phone while driving, even with a hands-free device, increases the risk of an accident. The risk goes up significantly if the driver is texting. An employee may feel like a loyal team member by making work-related calls from the driver's seat, but it's a form of loyalty that can kill. As Courtney Sanford's story attests, failure to be present while driving can cost human lives.

These examples suggest that to be present at work does not necessarily mean being fully committed to the job in every moment. Being a high-character employee shouldn't mean working like an automaton, with no opportunities for daydreaming, checking social media, making a personal call, or even goofing off a little. Some of my best ideas come when I'm not focused on my work. Creativity, the engine of progress, needs space to be born and grow.

But there's a big difference between an employee checking his Facebook page a couple of times during the day to see how many "likes" his latest post has gotten and constantly flitting between the Facebook and Excel tabs on his computer. Companies that block social media sites on their employees' computers don't solve the problem, because the sites are now easily accessible on smartphones.

Given the reality of today's world, as well as our need for breaks from time to time, I propose the following definition of presence in the workplace: *Presence is being committed to doing*

one's work by focusing on a single task for a reasonable period of time.
A "reasonable" period varies according to the task at hand and
the stakes involved in completing that task. You probably don't
want the surgeon performing your cardiac bypass to be checking
her smartphone. On the other hand, if the job isn't a life-or-death
matter, it's humane to allow an occasional respite from the steady
stream of work.

At the heart of presence is focus, the ability to concentrate on
one thing at a time. Focus is what separates people who are truly
present, like Ann Zuccardy, from multitaskers like Jane. Employees who are focused devote themselves to a single activity in a
given period, resulting in more efficient work with fewer mistakes. In his book *Focus,* Daniel Goleman suggests that this quality is akin to mindfulness, the practice of living in the moment.

Jon Kabat-Zinn, the author of *Wherever You Go, There You
Are,* has used mindfulness to treat chronic health conditions and
founded an influential stress clinic at the University of Massachu-
setts Medical School. Mindfulness was also responsible for the
profound transformation of *ABC News* anchor Dan Harris from
a drug-addicted, self-absorbed, deeply anxious young man to a
balanced, self-aware, and much kinder older man. Both focus
and mindfulness are broadly concerned with doing one thing at
a time, and employees who are focused or mindful reap rewards
for the people they serve as well as for themselves. Presence could
therefore also be called either *focus* or *mindfulness.*

A lecture called "The Power of Presence" by the business
thought leader Joe Calloway to members of the National Speakers Association convinced me to use *presence* as the term of art
here. Joe told a story about a closing speech he was about to give
to the insurance company Amerisure. On the evening before
Joe's speech, the company made its annual Loss Control Consultant of the Year award, and the recipient was asked to make a few

remarks after accepting the award. According to Joe, the recipient made many of the public-speaking mistakes that are the hallmark of an amateur. "He started with a bad joke, and he told it badly. He couldn't quite gather his thoughts. His physical delivery bordered on bizarre." At this point I wondered why Joe, a noted professional speaker, would take potshots at a guy who obviously wasn't as experienced as he is. But despite doing everything wrong, "this guy was *remarkable*," Joe said reverently. "He held that room, there wasn't a dry eye in the house, and he touched everybody's hearts. He had such presence it was palpable. If only I could have had that much the next day."

I want to be like that guy. Joe Calloway, who is greatly respected in the business world, uses presence to describe what others call focus or mindfulness, as does Eckhart Tolle, one of the most influential spiritual leaders in the world. On *60 Minutes*, correspondent Anderson Cooper asked Jon Kabat-Zinn if mindfulness means "being present." "That's exactly what it means," Kabat-Zinn replied. *Presence* is the title of a woefully underappreciated album by Led Zeppelin, but it is also the term we'll use for the tenth and final quality of high-character employees.

Presence is not, strictly speaking, a character trait in the moral sense, like the other nine qualities we've considered. But failing to be present makes it much harder to practice those other qualities. Courtney Sanford had many wonderful qualities, but by taking selfies and posting on Facebook while driving, she wasn't present when it mattered most. She didn't care properly for herself and others, and it cost her her life. Fully present people like Ann Zuccardy, on the other hand, demonstrate care in one of the most important ways possible: they do one thing at a time. They also do courageous things like asking for help when they need it, they're humble about their achievements, and they express gratitude regularly to the people who enrich their lives.

Listening and the Art of Being Present

One way that high-character employees demonstrate presence is by listening well. Because listening plays such a crucial role in business success, we'll give it special emphasis.

Suppose you're at a cocktail party and introduce yourself to someone you don't know. Let's call him Clyde.

You: Nice to meet you. How are you?

Clyde: Oh, what a day! Unbelievable. My alarm didn't go off, so I overslept, which meant I didn't have time to eat breakfast — I usually have at least eggs or some oatmeal and fresh fruit, maybe a decaf coffee — and my car didn't have much gas in it, so I went to fill it up, and I discovered I didn't have enough money in my checking account, so then I had to…"

Clyde doesn't notice that when you asked how he was doing, you were being polite. You didn't mean "Tell me everything that happened to you today." Nevertheless, you care about people, so you do your best to listen to Clyde ramble on, even though he lost you at the gas station. You ask a follow-up question or two. Again, you listen to the minutely detailed answers. "Eventually Clyde will stop talking about himself," you think, "and then maybe we can talk about something we're both interested in. Perhaps he'll even express a little interest in me!"

After Clyde finishes his third ramble, this one about a TV show he saw last night, you offer your own take on the program, but as soon as you begin speaking, Clyde barely stifles a yawn. Then he sees someone else at the party he'd rather talk to (or at) and excuses himself. That's the end of your encounter with Clyde.

Clyde doubtless has many fine qualities, perhaps even some that we've talked about in this book. But one quality Clyde appears to be grossly deficient in is listening well. Endlessly fascinated by the sound of his own voice, Clyde doesn't understand that a conversation is best when both people get a chance to be heard. It's not a monologue.

Clyde's dire listening skills stem from a failure to be present. Had Clyde been truly aware of you, he would have appreciated that you have a story or two to tell yourself, and he would have made a good-faith effort to pay attention to those stories, even if they weren't of great interest to him. But Clyde is so wrapped up in himself that he can't see beyond the borders of his own world.

The worst you can say about Clyde is that he's a big bore: rude, insensitive, lacking in social skills. But it's just a cocktail party, so Clyde's offenses aren't that significant. The real problems begin when poor listeners like Clyde come to work.

Managers Who Don't Listen Well

Silvia Aprosio is a human resources consultant and coach in Milan, Italy. She recently worked with a Fortune 100 company and told me about what can happen when an upper-level manager doesn't listen to a direct report. I'll refer to the manager as Federico and his direct report as Giulietta.

"Giulietta was charged with defining a new retail structure for the company," Silvia told me via Skype. "She spent a lot of time and effort researching the issue, writing a detailed report, and offering suggestions to Federico about how the business could improve the sales of its products in stores. Federico took none of her suggestions, and Giulietta was so upset, she screamed at him in the hallway." That struck me as an extreme reaction, so I asked Silvia, "Do you believe that Federico had an obligation to follow Giulietta's suggestions because of the work she did?"

"No," Silvia replied, "but he *did* have a responsibility to listen to her and to take her report seriously." Apparently Federico had a pattern of asking for suggestions from her and then ignoring them

212 THE GOOD ONES

completely. "That's not good management," Silvia observed. In other words, that's not what a high-character employee would do.

Federico, Silvia came to learn, paid little attention to anyone below him in the organization. He felt he knew everything he needed to know. Silvia recalled one of the tales from *1,001 Arabian Nights,* in which a pasha (boss) dresses like a beggar and goes to a tavern to hear what others are saying about him. Silvia believes executives and others in leadership positions should take the moral of that story seriously.

In the chapters on courage and gratitude, I referred to Ken Blanchard and Spencer Johnson's *One-Minute Manager* and its "praise down/criticize up" rule. That book also recommended that managers get out of their offices and regularly walk the floor to see what is happening on the front lines of their organizations. "In my consulting work over the years, I see executives becoming more and more detached from reality," Silvia noted. "They begin their careers wanting to become powerful, but at the end they are far removed from the real world." The simple act of listening to others is a corrective to this. And it doesn't have to involve changing your clothes.

The Benefits of Listening

Before Nancy Nebeker became middle school dean of the Waterford School in Sandy, Utah, she opened a pre-kindergarten school in Bangkok. "One of the teachers I hired wasn't doing a very good job," Nancy said. "She didn't come to work on time, wasn't prepared, and several times when I dropped in on her class, she looked like she was asleep. I'd never dealt with someone like that before, someone who wasn't motivated to perform. Her heart just wasn't in it." The school was for English-speaking children, and it wasn't easy to find qualified teachers in Thailand, especially in the middle of a term, so firing Stella, as I'll call her, wasn't an option.

The solution turned out to be straightforward. "I asked her questions about what she was doing and how she felt about what she was doing," Nancy told me. "Through a series of conversations, I didn't tell her what to do. Instead, I asked her anything and everything I could to draw her out, and through her responses offer my own perspective on what we were trying to achieve." The heart of the problem wasn't that Stella was bored or uninterested in the work but rather that she didn't know what she was expected to do. Although Stella had worked with young children, she had never taught pre-kindergarten before. It was only by listening carefully to Stella that Nancy discovered what was going on.

"The conversations weren't easy," Nancy said, "and I wish I could tell you that she changed overnight or even became my stellar teacher." That didn't happen. "But she did change, and I began to understand what she could bring to the classroom. By understanding what was troubling her, I was able to help her make progress. She felt inadequate to the job, and I never would have guessed that at the beginning."

This story illustrates that humility can be a critical component in listening. By giving up a degree of her authority or power over Stella, Nancy overcame a problem that seemed insurmountable. Circumstances forced her to work with the employee she had and to recalibrate her management style. Nancy Nebeker is one of the Good Ones because she is humble enough to put her ego aside, patient enough to explore the concerns of the people she manages, and willing to do something that neither Clyde nor Federico could be bothered to do: listen carefully to another person.

Becoming a Better Listener — and a Happier, More Successful Leader

Silvia Aprosio also told me about a second upper-level manager who was dismayed about his career. His division wasn't doing well, and he found it hard to relate to people in the organization. The company hired Silvia to coach the fellow, whom I'll call Vittorio. "His problem was the opposite of Federico's," Silvia said. "Vittorio spent too much time listening to the problems of other people and not enough time attuned to what was going on within him. He was surrounded by cacophony and couldn't tune out the noise."

Vittorio and Silvia met for the first time on December 23. "He said he had just a half an hour to talk because he was expected to go to the company Christmas party," Silvia told me, "but once he opened up, he kept going — for two and a half hours."

Silvia told Vittorio that he needed to make space for himself amid the chaos at work and suggested that he take a week off to focus on his own needs. He went to a beach in Mexico, didn't check his phone or email, and came back rejuvenated. He now pays attention to what his inner voice tells him, and both he and his division, he says, are better off.

There are two kinds of listening problems that prevent employees and their organizations from being at their best. Federico refused to listen to informed recommendations and alienated the people who could have helped him see things from another, possibly better, point of view. Vittorio spent too much time listening to others and became alienated from himself. Vittorio had the courage and humility to take advice about how to help himself, and he now feels more connected to his work and to other people. Federico doesn't believe he needs help and remains convinced that he always knows what's best. Whom would *you* rather work with?

Presence Is Being Fully Immersed in an Activity

When you cross a street or walk down stairs, do you consciously think about it? This is what Ann Zuccardy has to go through as a result of her brain injury:

It's very hard for me to process information when it's
coming from both directions, and that can get you run
over.... I['ve] developed this adaptation for crossing a
street: I scan the crowd, and I find the most responsible-
looking person. Often that's a mother with a small child.
Then I attach myself to them and follow them across the
street until I feel safe.

When I go downstairs, I grip the bannister with all
my might, and then I use my foot...to feel where I need
to step down.

Ann would be the first to tell you that there are many people
who face greater physical and psychological challenges than she
does. For some of them, crossing the street or walking down stairs
is impossible. But her story has a lot to teach us about the power
of presence.

To accomplish something that most of us take for granted,
Ann has to be completely focused on what she is doing. There are
serious, potentially fatal consequences to her if she isn't. She can't
afford to think about her work, or what her next meal is going to
be, or any of the myriad other things that float through our minds
when we're going from here to there. She is focused like a laser on
accomplishing the task at hand.

All of this is exhausting just to imagine, let alone execute.
What's striking about the way Ann tells her story is her joy.
I've never heard such a distressing experience related in such an
upbeat manner. Perhaps she was a joyful person before her accident; I didn't know her then. But I do know that this event made
her appreciate how every moment counts, how precious life is,
and how quickly it can be permanently altered. This realization
has prompted Ann to see and feel, in ways she had never been
prompted to do before, the vitality of every passing second.

Ann *has* to concentrate with all her might on simple chores.

You and I don't. But imagine what doing so might mean for both our productivity and the satisfaction we derive if we did our jobs with her degree of mindfulness. What are the implications for the workplace? Doing work means getting from A (a task that needs to be completed) to B (a task that has been completed). High-character employees recognize that the best way to get from A to B is to be fully present every step of the way, just as Ann Zuccardy is when she crosses the street.

Self-Awareness: The Secret to Being Present and Successful

Rick is a U.S. Navy judge advocate general (JAG). Rick's responsibilities include defending active members of the military against violations of the Uniform Code of Military Justice and other offenses. Most of the time his clients are grateful for his assistance, but recently an officer named Gordon tested Rick's ability to do his job well. Rick was assigned to defend Gordon against charges specified by Gordon's superior officer.

Gordon was going through a painful divorce at the time and took out his frustration on Rick. He challenged almost everything Rick said. Gordon's anger made it difficult for Rick to help him, because he refused to listen to what Rick had to say.

When civilian attorneys encounter a client like Gordon, they have the option of parting ways, but this generally isn't an option for military defense counsels. The more Gordon resisted Rick, the more Rick resented having to work with him, which didn't serve either of them well. Rick had to come up with a way of doing his job without becoming ensnared by Gordon's emotional issues.

The solution came when Rick was thinking about the time in college when he played a military prosecutor in Herman Wouk's play *The Caine Mutiny Court-Martial*. Rick's character was a really forceful, persistent guy, and he remembered how playing that role helped him become more confident in his life. So he thought, "What if I approached my work with Gordon the way I did that play? As an acting job?" If he could act the role of a calm, focused attorney, maybe it would prevent him from getting sidetracked by Gordon's hostility.

That's exactly what happened. The next time Gordon questioned Rick's advice, Rick told himself, "He's angry about his situation, not my competence." Rick became aware of the things that triggered his own emotional response, and by stepping outside of himself and looking at the situation dispassionately, he was able to stay grounded in the here and now. By staying the course, he was able to advise Gordon throughout the legal proceedings. (Rick declined to discuss the specific outcome, but suffice it to say it was favorable for his client.)

Rick still gets flummoxed from time to time with clients, but when that happens, he's aware of it, and he doesn't let it interfere with his job. By playing the part of a self-aware, fully present attorney, Rick has become one, and he is more successful — and personally satisfied — as a result.

Present Employees Are Desirable Colleagues

A reporter for ABC News named Dan Harris had a meltdown on live television. As he details in his book, *10% Happier,* a cocaine and Ecstasy habit he developed after covering the war in Afghanistan wreaked havoc on his neurological system. While reading the news on *Good Morning America,* he had a panic attack, and unable to speak clearly, he had to cut his segment short.

This incident prompted him to learn why he felt the need to self-medicate and how he could lead a healthier, more satisfying life. One of the things that got in the way of his being happy and productive, Dan says, was the constant mental chatter that so many of us have. His steady parade of thoughts wasn't about the here and now but, as Joni Mitchell lamented, "hoping for the future and worrying about the past." Dan discovered that the practice of meditation helped him to stay focused, become more productive, and, as the title of the book suggests, lead a happier life.

Before he began meditating, Dan was short-tempered, quick to anger, and prone to intense bouts of self-doubt and worry. What is noteworthy about Dan's transformation is not so much that he achieved success as we traditionally think about it — a more powerful and better-paid position at work — but that he was able to accept setbacks with equanimity and grace. He became a nicer person to be around, and the compassion he developed for others made him the colleague that others sought out for advice and friendship.

Dan would be the first to admit that you don't have to practice meditation daily to be a kind, considerate employee who makes positive contributions to the workplace. It turns out, though, that meditation strengthens the prefrontal cortex, the part of the brain that controls emotions. Dan's ability to be present, which for him and many others flows from the practice of meditation, makes him one of the Good Ones.

Distracted Employees Are Bad for Business

Last week I was at a trade show and approached a vendor whose service I had been considering signing up for. The service has a five-figure price tag, so I needed to know exactly what I would be getting for my money. A senior representative of the company greeted me and began telling me about the benefits of the service (without, I may add, asking me anything about what I needed it for). Within twenty seconds, he glanced at his smartphone, looked back up at me, and then called out to someone he knew in the vicinity. Then he went back to his spiel.

It was a busy trade show, so I didn't want to begrudge him a moment to reach out to a friend. But throughout his pitch, he kept looking at his phone and glancing around the room. The message was clear: "I have things I'd rather be doing than talking to you." It was an odd style of selling, because his competitors were just a few booths away. He gave me some of the company's literature, encouraged me to read it, and warmly greeted his friend who had approached us. No sale.

In her *Wall Street Journal* article with the challenging title "Workplace Distractions: Here's Why You Won't Finish This Article," Rachel Emma Silverman explains that contemporary workers face an increasing number of distractions that make it difficult to focus. The fourteen thousand employees of Intel's Software and Services group "were concerned that they weren't getting time to think deeply about problems because they spent much of their time keeping up with day-to-day tasks." Workers at Robins Air Force Base in Georgia were repairing fewer than 50 percent of planes on time because they were juggling too many tasks at once.

Presence, as I defined it earlier, is being committed to doing one's work by focusing on a single task for a reasonable period of time. All sorts of distractions, work-related and personal, work against this: handling email and text messages, chatting to colleagues in an open office, running several applications at once, and the lure of Facebook and Twitter. Lacy Roberson, eBay's director of learning and organizational development, calls the constant stream of interruptions "an epidemic." And as the air force situation demonstrates, it doesn't take electronic distractions to hamper presence. Simply being asked to do too many things at once can be just as detrimental. Presence and productivity are inextricably bound together.

Obstacles to Presence
and How High-Character Employees Deal with Them

Technology Feeds Distraction

The Buster Keaton quotation presented previously talks about the impossibility of doing two things at once well — and it dates from the beginning of the twentieth century. Keaton couldn't have imagined what the future held: emails, texts, websites, multiple open applications, and phone calls all vying for our attention.

Some argue that multitasking actually makes us more productive. In "The Case for Multitasking," Vangelis Souitaris, a professor at London's Cass Business School, and B. M. Marcello Maestro, managing director of the New York investment firm Bravemarket, studied nearly two hundred executives and determined that companies whose teams tended to multitask performed better financially than companies where monotasking was the norm. The entrepreneur David Silverman and researchers at the Chinese University of Hong Kong make their own cases for the power of multitasking. But the overwhelming majority of psychological research and business articles make a convincing case that multitasking generally diminishes rather than enhances productivity.

Of course, there are some circumstances when monotasking isn't an option. If you have an urgent memo to write but also need to be on an unrelated conference call, you have to manage to do both. Most of the time, though, we have a choice. Courtney Sanford had a choice, and the one she made — posting to her Facebook account while driving — killed her.

People who are truly present come up with strategies for minimizing or eliminating distractions from their work — and their rest. Quentin Tarantino doesn't allow anyone on his movie sets to use smartphones. Ana Veciana-Suarez, who writes a column on family issues for the *Miami Herald*, sets a strict limit on reading and responding to email and checking her social media: twenty to thirty minutes every morning. "Otherwise," she says, "I'll say to myself, 'Oh, I'll just be a few more minutes,' but it's never just a few minutes." Nancy Nebeker, the educator, has phone-free Fridays at her school for students and staff alike. Mark Bittman speaks of taking a "secular Sabbath" and unplugging on the weekends. Following suit, Jon Taplin, the film producer and professor, doesn't turn on his computer or check email at all on Sunday.

Overload and Fatigue

"There never seems to be enough time to do the things you want to do," sang the late Jim Croce in "Time in a Bottle." It's a love song, but this lyric could be the motto of anyone who has a job today. No matter how well we manage our time — making to-do lists, distinguishing between the urgent and the important, giving each project the attention it deserves — we feel as though we're always behind.

When we have too much to do, our decisionmaking becomes compromised as the day goes on or as our decisions pile up. That's the conclusion of Roy F. Baumeister, Kathleen Vohs, Mark Heitmann, and other social scientists who have studied the phenomenon of decision fatigue. Computers function as well at 5 PM as at 9 AM. Human beings, however, can accomplish only so much in a day before losing the ability to function well. One study showed that judges were more likely to grant a prisoner parole if the case was adjudicated in the morning. Prisoners who had committed the same or lesser offenses but who appeared before the parole board in the afternoon were less likely to be released early. This disparity violates a basic rule of fairness — treating like cases alike and unalike cases unalike — and decision fatigue appears to be the culprit.

It's hard to be fully present after a long day and in a state of mental and physical exhaustion. It's even harder if we haven't eaten properly. "That's why the truly wise don't restructure the company at 4 PM," notes the science writer John Tierney. "They don't make major commitments during the cocktail hour. And if a decision must be made late in the day, they know not to do it on an empty stomach." Or, as Roy Baumeister says, "The best decision makers are the ones who know when *not* to trust themselves."

Oppressive Bosses

Jake is a management consultant at a large firm. He loves his work and for years has enjoyed good relationships with clients. I've known Jake for a long time, and he isn't a complainer. One of the things I've always admired about him, in fact, is how he always finds the good in people. So when he went on at length during one of our recent phone conversations about how oppressive his boss has been, I took notice.

"Last week, Theodore insulted me in front of the other people at the office. It would have been bad enough if he talked to me that way privately. But the way he did it was humiliating." I asked Jake to elaborate. "For one thing, when he criticizes me, he doesn't focus on a specific thing I've done wrong. He'll say, 'You never do it right.' I know that's not true, because if I were that incompetent, I would have been let go a long time ago. He also calls me names. Not obscene ones, but they're still insulting."

I asked Jake if he had complained to HR about Theodore's behavior. "Yes, I did — last year. The problem is that Theodore found out about it, and he's been even nastier to me ever since."

Because Theodore hasn't engaged in the kind of conduct, like sexual or racial harassment, that could rightfully get him fired, and the team he manages does well for the firm, it's not likely that he'll be leaving the company anytime soon. But his behavior does the organization no favors. "After one of Theodore's tirades, I find it hard to focus," Jake told me. "I'll obsess over something he's done or said, and then I realize I've haven't been doing what I'm supposed to be doing." This is the antithesis of being present at work.

Jake compared Theodore's degrading management style with that of his former boss, Molly. "Now there was a true gem," Jake said. "Molly never raised her voice. If she had a criticism to make, it was done in the spirit of helping me be as successful as I could be. She cared about me, and as a result, I worked hard. It was easy to be focused, because she made coming to work fun."

Jake is one of the Good Ones, but bosses like Theodore make it hard for employees like him to be at their best. He's had enough of Theodore's management style and is looking for a new job. That may take care of Jake's problem, but his current employer will have to spend time, money, and effort to find a replacement. No matter what Theodore's positive qualities may be, a more respectful approach to management would allow the people who report to him to be fully present in their jobs and thus be more productive, more satisfied, and more likely to stick around.

Evaluating Presence

Unless a job candidate is fiddling with his or her smartphone throughout the interview, determining the candidate's commitment to being present is tough but not impossible. The following questions may provide some guidance.

Tell me about a time when you were distracted at work and dealt with the distraction successfully.

In Homer's *Odyssey*, the hero, Odysseus, tells the crew of his ship that they're about to sail by a group of dangerous women known as the Sirens, whose beautiful music lures unsuspecting sailors to their deaths. Odysseus orders his crew to put beeswax in their ears, tie him to the mast of the ship, and keep him tied there, no matter how much he begs them to let him go. Odysseus's novel method for protecting himself and his crew from the deadly allure of the Sirens is successful.

This scene is the best illustration I know of the potential dangers of allowing our passions to take us off course. There are lots of responses to this first question that would reveal the candidate's commitment to being present that don't necessarily involve earplugs (though those may indeed be the solution if the distraction is construction work outside the office or noisy coworkers inside).

A modern-day way to avoid distractions that Odysseus would approve of is software that blocks access to distracting websites. I use two versions of this, both made by a company in Chapel Hill, North Carolina, called Eighty Percent Solutions. One version, Freedom, blocks all internet access; the other, Anti-Social, can be programmed to block social media sites like Facebook and Twitter. You determine how much uninterrupted time you want on your computer — you can specify up to eight hours — and then your computer will thwart your urge to check your Facebook page or Twitter feed during that time. A job candidate who talks about using such software is someone who takes his or her work seriously, understands how disruptive distractions can be, and does what it takes to be fully present and focused.

Others use yoga or meditation to help them develop focus. Sometimes, however, disturbances come from without rather than within — overly chatty coworkers, needy bosses or direct reports, or office noise, for example — and earplugs aren't a practical solution. If an applicant responds that a problem with a colleague or family member posed a distraction, I'd hope to hear something along the lines of, "I spent some time talking with that person and eventually worked through the problem." Imagine that — going right to the source of the distraction and resolving it directly.

Do you expect your direct reports to have business conversations on the phone while they're driving?

This question helps the interviewer learn two things about the job candidate: how he or she feels about smartphones and driving, and how committed the candidate is to allowing team members to have a boundary between professional and personal life.

A study by the National Safety Council showed that 80 percent of Americans believe that driving while using a hands-free device for calling is safe. But even these devices increase the risk of an accident, according to research by the American Automobile Association's Foundation for Traffic Safety and the Virginia Tech Transportation Institute. The distraction that causes the problem isn't just the conversation itself but all of the activities that go along with receiving or placing the call. Texting while driving involves taking one's eyes off the road, which is why an increasing number of states have laws banning this practice, but it turns out that even the use of hands-free devices is potentially deadly.

Once cars can drive themselves, a development that may not be too far off, having a phone conversation behind the wheel will not be a life-or-death matter. But until that day comes, smart employers will not allow their employees to accept or make phone calls while driving, even with hands-free devices. Employers who want to be considered fair will recognize that there is a time and a place for having phone conversations and will give their employees what is due to them: the freedom to get from A to B without increasing the risk of harm to anyone. Taking business calls while driving is irresponsible. High-character managers will not expect employees to do this, and employees who value their lives and the lives of other drivers will not do it either.

Talk about a time when you didn't listen well or pay attention at work. What were the consequences?

Like some of the questions in previous chapters, this may be hard to answer on the spot. For one thing, we don't like to dwell on our failures. And if you're not paying attention or listening to someone, how can you know what you missed? After all, your mind was somewhere else.

The point of the question, though, is to find out how the candidate dealt with a situation where he or she *should* have been present but wasn't, and that's something everyone can relate to. For example, yesterday afternoon I took a break from writing this chapter on presence to do the dishes. But I was thinking about something else when I was putting an item aside to dry, and I knocked over a container that was sitting on the stove. The lid flew into the air and landed behind the oven. What could have been a pleasant few minutes away from my computer screen turned into a wild goose chase, frantic texts to my wife, and far too much time devoted to recovering the lost gizmo (although I wound up with a great anecdote for this chapter). I learned that even the high-minded pursuit of writing about presence doesn't mean much unless the writer puts those ideas into action, and that it's valuable to focus and be mindful even when doing something as mundane as cleaning.

SUMMARY

Presence is a commitment to doing one's work by focusing on a single task for a reasonable period of time.

Employees who are present are good listeners because they concentrate on the person speaking instead of on their own concerns.

Technology, work overload, and oppressive bosses are formidable but not insurmountable obstacles to presence.

CONCLUSION

Character may be an unusual topic of conversation in business, but as these true stories reveal, character is observable, subject to evaluation, and indispensable. The ten character traits we've examined are qualities that smart organizations value in their job candidates, employees, and managers. Doing so won't guarantee that the people who work for a company will always make the best decisions, but it increases the likelihood that they will.

It's time to place character front and center in our thinking about business in the twenty-first century. The Good Ones do. How about you?

CALL TO ACTION

The material you've just read in this book is completely worthless unless you put it into action. The following suggestions will help you do so, wherever you work and whatever you do.

For Employers

1. Incorporate the ten qualities of high-character employees into the core competencies that your organization expects from its employees.
2. When you prepare a job description, discuss character as an essential component of the position, not something that adds value to it. Doing the job well has to mean acting with honor and integrity, not merely hitting sales numbers or closing deals. In job postings, mention up front that you're looking for

people of high character. Don't be afraid to use words like *honest, fair, ethical, honorable,* and *integrity* in the ad.

3. Add some or all of the ten qualities of high-character employees to your company's mission, vision, and values statements, and explain why successful applicants will be in alignment with these values. Make it clear that your organization considers knowledge and skill to be necessary but not sufficient. High character is also an essential element of employment.

4. The stories in this book illustrate why high-character people are crucial to a company's success. Gather stories like these from your organization and present them at staff meetings. Every year the CEO of a major home improvement company shares with employees the stories of five high-character people like Emiliano, who tracked down the owner of a $15,000 diamond ring that he discovered in a store's parking lot. Emiliano received a prestigious award and a bonus, for which his colleagues gave him a roaring standing ovation. The takeaway? "I want to be like him."

5. The ten qualities of high-character employees should be a critical factor for making hiring, promotion, and termination decisions at every level of the company. In both job interviews and performance reviews, use the questions at the end of each chapter to help you evaluate, in behavioral terms, the character of applicants or employees seeking raises or promotions. The goal is to discover the extent to which the person's conduct is consistent with the company's values.

For Job Candidates

1. Before applying for a position with an organization, study its mission and vision statements and its code of ethics. Connect with current and former employees to learn more about the company's culture. Look for examples from the company's website, the news, and business literature that describe how the company has put its values into practice.

2. During your interview, emphasize that you're not only highly qualified in your field but that, as someone who takes ethics seriously, you are committed to doing the right thing every time, everywhere. Be prepared to cite the examples of the company's commitment to integrity that you researched. Use stories from your own experience, like the ones in this book, to illustrate how honesty, accountability, and the like were critical in helping you deliver results in the previous jobs you've had.

3. Send a thank-you note after the interview. Mention some of the company's values and reiterate that you are deeply committed to upholding these values in everything you say and do. Sending a hand-written thank-you note instead of an email is an especially nice — and rare — touch.

Very few, if any, of your competitors will be saying or doing anything like this. Simply mentioning ethics, honor, or character in your communications will set you apart from the rest, and when you back up these statements with evidence that demonstrates that you are a person of high character and how this commitment has helped you deliver results, you will rightly jump to the top of the company's short list of contenders.

For Employees Seeking a Raise or Promotion

How can you convince your employer to give you the raise or promotion you know you deserve? Demonstrating how your knowledge and skill have benefited the company isn't enough.

1. Well before you plan to ask for a salary increase or higher position, keep a list of statements your supervisor and other leaders in the organization have made, and a description of things they've done, that speak to the company's commitment to honor and integrity.

2. Create a file that contains raves you've received from clients, coworkers, online contacts, and others that testify to your honesty, courage, and other aspects of your character and show how your conduct has benefited others. If you make a habit of referring to character in the recommendations that you write on LinkedIn or elsewhere, you'll create an example for others to follow.

3. During your performance review, emphasize that you've not only done superior work, but that you've also consistently demonstrated a commitment to doing the right thing, which has led to better results. Cite the examples from step 1 and use another personal story or two to show how your actions align with the company's values.

Please let me know how this call to action has worked for you. Write to me at bruce@theethicsguy.com or via my website, TheEthicsGuy.com, and I will send you a thank-you gift.

ACKNOWLEDGMENTS

This book would be shorter than the pamphlets the flight attendant distributes to passengers in the movie *Airplane!* without the generosity of so many people who agreed to be interviewed and allowed me to tell their stories. These inspiring men and women are, in alphabetical order of their first names: Alan Murray, Alan Paul Price, Alan Tecktiel, Alexander Shermansong, Alexandra Troy, Allen Dyer, Ana Cristina Reymundo, Ana Veciana-Suarez, Andi Sciacca, Andrea Koehler, Ann Zuccardy, B. David Jaffe, Ben Eubanks, Ben Baldwin, Bill Hughes, Bill Sailer, Bill Treasurer, Brenda Harry, Cara Lemieux, Cari Dorman, Chris Webb, Christine Harkins Reid, Chuck Gallagher, Craig B. Lamb, Craig Kappmeier, Darius Norell, David Dawit Searles, David Mielke, Deb Saunders, Diane McCullough, Don Feldmann, Ed Askinazi, Ed Krow, Eileen Gray, Eryn Swenson, Fred Smith, Gail Stewart-Evans, Genise Wade, Gregory B. Sadler, Janice Piacente, Jeffrey Hayzlett, Jeremy C. Park, Jerry Kitchens, Jess Todtfeld,

Joan Ceinski, John A. Byrne, John Geenen, John Spence, Jonathan Taplin, Karen Jacobsen, Kenneth W. Meyer, SPHR, Kevin Kennemer, Kim Scholes, Kirk LaPointe, Marc Beshar, Mark Fogel, Mark Lagasse, Marlene Shea, Matt Paese, Nancy Smith Nebeker, Paula Smith, Peter Sarkis, Philip B. Davis, Randi B. Glinsky, Roger Chiang, Russ Hovendick, Scott Erker, PhD, Sharon Dunbar, Silvia Aprosio, Simone Stewart, Steve Werner, Tara Fitzgerald, Terry Brock, Tom Donahue, Val Wright, and Zoe Olsberg. Although I don't quote directly from all of the interviews, every one of them was fascinating and helpful.

Thanks also to Elizabeth Damewood Goucher of Longwood Editors for her superb, cheerful assistance with some of the research. Wizard of Homes extraordinaire Triin Härma and Meg Owen of Get It Together Organizers kept my office in tip-top shape, and Help a Reporter Out did indeed help me at the beginning of this project. I met the majority of the people I interviewed through LinkedIn, so I'm happily indebted to this outstanding service.

I'm especially grateful for the love and support of my friends Ed Askinazi, B. David Joffe, Gary Sunshine, Jess Todtfeld, Jeff Clarkson, Jill DeForte, Kaori Kitao, Mark Lagasse, Peter Sarkis, Patricia O'Connell, Richard A. Solomon, Ron Karr, Steve Werner, and Will Hood; and my family, Carlee Daylor, Judy Bancroft, Liz Horne, Michael Horne, Rachel Weinstein, Sammy Daylor, Sharon Bancroft, my mother Sheila Weinstein, and Will Bancroft. Even though my father, George Weinstein, is no longer with us, his spirit is always with me, and he also gave me a great story for the chapter on honesty!

Five people merit special praise for their extraordinary help in reviewing earlier drafts of this book. They are Alan Tecktiel, Erika Büky, Jason Gardner, Kristen Bancroft, and Robert Timko. Alan Tecktiel gave me a wealth of useful information about how HR management works. Erika Büky's astute observations and questions helped me to strengthen and clarify many key points throughout the book, and Jason Gardner once again offered insightful suggestions for improving this material. Editing books is similar to dealing with customers at airports: you hear only the complaints. That's one of the reasons why I decided to dedicate this book to Jason. But the main reason is that he is one of the Good Ones and deserves to be recognized as such. Bob gave me the idea for this book when he reviewed my previous work *Ethical Intelligence*. He noted that I briefly referred to courage as a component of ethical intelligence but didn't discuss moral virtue in any depth. That's what prompted me to reflect on the role of virtue in professional life, so thank you for that excellent observation, Bob!

I owe a huge debt of gratitude to my brilliant wife, Kristen. Besides putting up with the long gestation of this work (which is a nice way of saying she tolerated two years of my being a grouch), Kristen provided an invaluable perspective on corporate life, since she is a senior compliance officer at a major financial institution and also has an intellect that far surpasses mine.

In the film version of Rodgers and Hammerstein's *The Sound of Music,* Maria sings that she "must have done something good" as a child because she enjoys so many riches in her life. If this section of the book had a theme song, it would be that one, because all of the people listed above generously and graciously gave their time, effort, and insight to this project. I thank them all from the bottom of my heart.

ENDNOTES

Introduction

2   *Employees who are actively disengaged:* Gallup, "State of the American Workplace," September 22, 2014, www.gallup.com/services/176708/state-american-workplace.aspx.

2   *The typical organization loses 5 percent of revenues:* Association of Certified Fraud Examiners, *Report to the Nations on Occupational Fraud and Abuse: 2014 Global Fraud Study,* www.acfe.com/rttn-summary.aspx, accessed January 12, 2015.

2   *Workplace violence:* Eric Goldschein and Kim Bhasin, "14 Surprising Ways Employees Cost Their Companies Billions in the Workplace," *Business Insider,* November 29, 2011, www.businessinsider.com/surprising-costs-to-the-work-place-2011-11.

2   *"Some companies don't think it's important":* Panel discussion, "The ROI of Ethical Leadership in Business," BB&T Center for Ethical Business Leadership, Mike Cottrell College of Business, University of North Georgia, September 18, 2014. www.youtube.com/watch?v=AwRCcrbEW-o.

2   *"Sometimes companies are reluctant":* Author interview with John Spence, April 11, 2014.

3 *Even if companies do acknowledge:* Alan Tecktiel, personal communication, August 14, 2014.
7 *West Indian Licorice Mocha Delight:* I wish I could claim that I made up this flavor of ice cream, but that distinction belongs to Everett Greenbaum and Jim Fritzell, who wrote "A Date with Gomer," season 4, episode 105 of *The Andy Griffith Show,* aired November 25, 1963. See Dale Robinson and David Fernandes, *The Definitive Andy Griffith Show Reference,* (Jefferson, NC: McFarland & Company, 1996), 112.
8 *Dan Harris talks about:* See Dan Harris, *10% Happier: How I Tamed the Voice in My Head, Reduced Stress Without Losing My Edge, and Found Self-Help That Actually Works* (New York: It Books, 2014).
9 *Yet if Joe doesn't change:* Thanks to Alan Tecktiel for making this observation.
11 *We don't always do:* Nor do we always do what we should do. My parents taught me that if a stranger threatened me and asked for my wallet, I should give it to them without hesitation. That made sense: life is worth a lot more than the contents of our wallets. But on one sunny day in Amsterdam, in front of a crowded concert hall, three men approached me. One asked for the time and then came close and said, "I have a gun. Give me your wallet, or I'll shoot you." Impulsively I pushed him away with my umbrella and ran. He ran after me, but I outran him! Was that the right or smart thing to do? Probably not. I'm sure my parents would say I should have just given him my wallet and not taken the risk I did.

   Of course, it's possible that I perceived that running would be the safe option. As Malcolm Gladwell suggests in *Blink: The Power of Thinking without Thinking* (New York: Back Bay Books, 2007), we sometimes make good decisions instinctively, based on the way our subconscious minds rapidly assess a situation.
11 *"One bad seed":* Quoted in Sarah Max, "Uncertain about Hiring, Some Companies Try 'Test Drives,'" *New York Times,* September 10, 2014, www.nytimes.com/2014/09/11/business/smallbusiness/uncertain -about-hiring-some-companies-try-test-drives.html.
11 *Jon Bischke:* Ibid.
13 *How rarely prospective employers contact him:* Interview with Alan Murray, August 6, 2013. Some employees who have been fired may not disclose this fact, so prospective employers wouldn't be in a position to contact people like Alan in the first place.
13 *A book that had a big influence:* Jay Johnson, "The Playmaker: Bob Beaudine," *D,* October 2006, www.dmagazine.com/publications /d-ceo/2006/october/the-playmaker.

16 *"Who should I be?":* I learned this distinction from the theologian William F. May, who was one of my professors at Georgetown University's Kennedy Institute of Ethics and the author of *The Physician's Covenant: Images of the Healer in Medical Ethics* (Louisville, KY: Westminster John Knox Press, 2000).

20 *Where an American executive might say "no":* Stuart Freedman, "6 Things You Need to Know about Doing Business in Japan," *Business Insider,* June 3, 2014, http://www.businessinsider.com/6-things-to-know-about -business-in-japan-2014–6.

Chapter One: Honesty

27 *I wanted to know why Brenda didn't keep the money:* Interview with Deborah Saunders, March 24, 2014.

27 *I called Brenda:* Interview with Brenda Harry, May 9, 2014.

28 *How many people would do what Brenda did:* Unfortunately, no other employer will have the opportunity to hire Brenda Harry, because she retired in late 2014.

29 *"What if my son were in the navy?":* Interview with Cari Dorman, February 28, 2014.

29 *An employee's passion for the truth:* Interview with Ken Meyer, February 11, 2014.

30 *"All you have to do":* This video and accompanying text helped me to understand what is involved in inspecting fire extinguishers and exactly what the crooked vendor was asking Marvin to overlook: www.fire -extinguisher101.com/careandmaintenance.html.

32 *Knowing when to hold 'em:* "The Gambler," words and music by Don Schlitz (Sony/ATV, 1978).

35 *"No second acts":* F. Scott Fitzgerald, *The Love of the Last Tycoon,* ed. Matthew J. Bruccoli (New York: Scribner's, 1995).

35 *Chuck Gallagher transformed the poor choices:* Interview with Chuck Gallagher, March 11, 2014.

37 *A young man named David: Inventing David Geffen,* written, produced and directed by Susan Lacy, PBS, aired November 20, 2012, www.pbs .org/wnet/americanmasters/episodes/david-geffen/film-inventing -david-geffen/2361.

Chapter Two: Accountability

47 *"I'm going to do what I say I'm going to do":* Interview with Karen Jacobsen, April 7, 2014.

49　*Diana Mekota, a recent college graduate:* Janet H. Cho, "Job Bank Head Kelly Blazek Apologizes after Her Rejection Emails Go Viral," *Plain Dealer* (Cleveland), February 25, 2014, www.cleveland.com/business /index.ssf/2014/02/job_bank_head_kelly_blazeks_sc.html.

50　*The ethical issues in this story:* Janet H. Cho, "Kelly Blazek Again Shuts Down Job Bank Twitter Account; A Third Rejected Job Seeker Speaks Out," *Plain Dealer,* February 26, 2014, updated March 6, 2014, www .cleveland.com/business/index.ssf/2014/02/kelly_blazek_restarts_her _job_bank_twitter_account_with_an_apology_and_the_hashtag _letcitydown.html#incart_flyout_news. See also Janet H. Cho, "Kelly Blazek Returns Her 2013 Communicator of the Year Award after Social Media Backlash," *Plain Dealer,* March 05, 2014, updated March 6, 2014, www.cleveland.com/business/index.ssf/2014/03/kelly_blazek_returns _her_2013_communicator_of_the_year_award_after_social_media _backlash.html.

50　*Other recipients:* Ibid.

51　*"With great power":* This saying is variously attributed to Stan Lee (creator of Spider-Man), Superman, Richard Nixon, Franklin Delano Roosevelt, Voltaire, and Jesus. See thread on *Yahoo! Answers,* answers. yahoo.com/question/index?qid=20070107135519AAUe5TB, accessed January 12, 2015.

51　*Some of the Good Ones handle their work-related frustration:* See David Shipley and Will Schwalbe, *Send: Why People Email So Badly and How to Do It Better* (New York: Vintage Books, 2010).

53　*"Action-oriented":* Ken Sundheim, "15 Traits of the Ideal Employee," *Forbes.com,* April 2, 2013, www.forbes.com/sites/kensundheim /2013/04/02/15-traits-of-the-ideal-employee.

54　*"Accountability":* Kevin Daum, "5 Desirable Traits of Great Employees," *Inc.com,* August 28, 2013, www.inc.com/kevin-daum/5-tests-hiring -best-employees.html.

55　*May enhance retention and promote creativity:* "The Higher Purpose of Doodling," *CBS News Sunday Morning,* January 19, 2014, www.cbsnews .com/videos/the-higher-purpose-of-doodling.

56　*A study conducted at Bentley University:* Bentley University, *The PreparedU Project: An In-depth Look at Millennial Preparedness for Today's Workforce,* January 29, 201, 15, www.bentley.edu/files/prepared /1.29.2013_BentleyU_Whitepaper_Shareable.pdf. I learned about this study from Rob Asghar, "Study: Millennials and Employers Disagree on Path to Success," *Forbes.com,* January 28, 2014, www.forbes.com

/sites/robasghar/2014/01/28/study-millennials-and-employers
-disagree-on-path-to-success.

56 *"Luxury, bad manners, contempt for authority":* Thanks to Garson
O'Toole, quote investigator, for discovering the source of this quotation,
which is often mistakenly attributed to Socrates, quoteinvestigator
.com/2010/05/01/misbehaving-children-in-ancient-times.

56 *It's a Wonderful Life,* written by Frances Goodrich, Albert Hackett, Jo
Swerling, and Frank Capra; based on the story "The Greatest Gift" by
Philip Van Doren Stern; directed by Frank Capra (RKO Radio Pictures,
1946).

57 *"Hype artists":* Author interview with Jonathan Taplin, September 10,
2013.

59 *An internal investigation revealed:* Gretchen Morgenson, "A Vow to End
Hollow Nods and Salutes," *New York Times,* June 7, 2014, www.nytimes
.com/2014/06/08/business/gretchen-morgenson-on-the-problems
-at-gm.html.

62 *Managers spend almost 17 percent of their time:* Tiffany Hus, "Managers
Spend Almost a Day a Week on Slacker Workers, Study Says," *Los
Angeles Times* online, November 10, 2012, articles.latimes.com/2012
/nov/10/business/la-fi-bad-employees-20121110.

62 *Actively disengaged employees:* Gallup, "State of the American Workplace."

62 *Even a few errant employees:* Robert Sutton, "How a Few Bad Apples
Ruin Everything," *Wall Street Journal* online, October 24, 2011, www
.wsj.com/articles/SB10001424052970203499704576622550325233260.

Chapter Three: Care

67 *Scarface:* Written by Oliver Stone, directed by Brian De Palma (Columbia Pictures, 1983).

69 *"A servant-leader focuses":* Robert K. Greenleaf, *Servant Leadership: A
Journey into the Nature of Legitimate Power and Greatness* (New York:
Paulist Press, 2002 [originally published in 1977]).

71 *The English word* engagement: See *Online Etymology Dictionary,* www
.etymonline.com/index.php?term=engagement; Dictionary.com,
dictionary.reference.com/browse/engagement; Oxford Dictionaries,
www.oxforddictionaries.com/us/definition/american_english
/engagement.

71 *As Biro notes:* Meghan M. Biro, "Employee Engagement Is a Leadership
Commitment," *Forbes.com,* March 30, 2014, www.forbes.com/sites

/meghanbiro/2014/03/30/employee-engagement-is-a-leadership
-commitment.

71 *Only 30% of U.S. employees"*: Randall Beck and Jim Harter, "Why Great
Managers Are So Rare," Gallup Business, March 25, 2014, business
journal.gallup.com/content/167975/why-great-managers-rare.aspx.

71 *Employee engagement is linked to "higher profitability"*: Ibid.

72 *"The most important way to have people engaged"*: "Are Companies That
Value Employees More Successful?" reported by Martha Teichner, produced by David Rothman, *CBS News Sunday Morning*, August 31, 2014,
www.cbsnews.com/news/are-companies-that-value-employees
-more-successful.

72 *"Over the past ten years"*: Ibid.

73 *People who feel good are up to 12 percent more productive:* Andrew J.
Oswald, Eugenio Proto, and Daniel Sgroi, "Happiness and Productivity," *Journal of Labor Economics* (forthcoming, October 2015), www2
.warwick.ac.uk/fac/soc/economics/staff/eproto/workingpapers
/happinessproductivity.pdf.

I learned about this research from Emily Kuklinski, "Happy
Demeanor Will Make Life More Productive," *Daily Nebraskan,* October
2, 2014, www.dailynebraskan.com/opinion/kuklinski-happy-demeanor
-will-make-life-more-productive/article_6a093228–49f3–11e4-bd92
–0017a43b2370.html.

73 *Significant savings in health insurance costs:* "Healthy Employees =
Healthy Profits," *Business in the Community,* February 2009, webarchive
.nationalarchives.gov.uk/20130128102031/ www.dwp.gov.uk/docs
/hwwb-healthy-people-healthy-profits.pdf. I learned about this publica-
tion from Oswald et al., "Happiness and Productivity," 2.

76 *There's another way to generate:* Fred Smith, personal communication,
May 12, 2014.

77 *It also helps if your company:* Thanks to Alan Tecktiel for this observation.

77 *Employees with a healthy lifestyle:* Centers for Disease Control and Prevention, "Workplace Health Promotion," www.cdc.gov/workplace
healthpromotion/businesscase/benefits/productivity.html, accessed
January 5, 2015.

79 *Caring employees stay home:* In my previous book, *Ethical Intelligence,*
I also talked about the issue of going to work sick, but from a different
perspective.

80 *The drudgery of working on an assembly line:* The other classic comic take

on factory life is Charlie Chaplin's film *Modern Times*. If you've never seen this magnificent work of art, I urge you to do so.

80 *Bosses like Bernadette:* Author interview with Jess Todtfeld, April 21, 2014.

82 *"I told the client about my condition":* It's troubling that the client would be impressed, rather than concerned, by a speaker who is willing to come to an engagement when he has the flu. I understand that the client might balk at having to find a replacement at the last minute, but isn't that preferable to putting members of the audience at risk of becoming ill?

84 *The only thing she can't do well is cook:* Apparently the director of *Woman of the Year,* George Stevens, and the producer, Joseph L. Mankiewicz, added poor cooking skills to Tess Harding's character so that she would get her "comeuppance." Mary Anne Melear, "Woman of the Year," *Turner Classic Movies* online, www.tcm.com/this-month /article/31487|0/Woman-of-the-Year.html.

85 *Greed and contempt for customers:* Greg Smith, "Why I Am Leaving Goldman Sachs," *New York Times,* March 14, 2012, www.nytimes .com/2012/03/14/opinion/why-i-am-leaving-goldman-sachs.html. This is the source of all Smith's quotations here. See also Greg Smith, *Why I Left Goldman Sachs* (New York: Grand Central Publishing, 2012).

86 *How a successful airline decided:* Thanks to Phil Davis, who took the workshop with me and reminded me of this anecdote.

Chapter Four: Courage

91 *Allan McDonald:* "Failure is Your Friend," *Freakonomics,* podcast, June 4, 2014, freakonomics.com/2014/06/04/failure-is-your-friend-full -transcript.

92 *"A ship in harbor":* There is debate about the source of this quotation, but the research by Garson O'Toole, the Quote Investigator, is substantial and concludes that the author is John A. Shedd and that it appeared in his 1928 collection of sayings, *Salt from My Attic,* quoteinvestigator .com/2013/12/09/safe-harbor/ accessed January 5, 2015. I first saw this quotation on a poster at the fast-food restaurant where I worked in high school, which I discuss in the chapter on fairness.

92 *Courageous employees:* On his radio show *A Prairie Home Companion,* Garrison Keillor includes product endorsements by the mythical manufacturer of Powdermilk Biscuits, a food product that "gives shy persons the strength to get up and do what needs to be done." There may be no better description of what it means to be courageous in the workplace.

93   *For thirty years, Alexandra Troy:* Author interview with Alexandra Troy, May 2, 2014.

95   *Lois Wallace:* Daniel E. Slotnik, "Lois Wallace, a Respected Agent of Prominent Authors, Dies at 73," *New York Times,* April 18, 2014, www.nytimes.com/2014/04/19/business/media/lois-wallace-a -respected-agent-of-prominent-authors-dies-at-73.html.

95   *What Would Nixon Do?:* Ben Stein, "Lois Wallace, RIP," *American Spectator,* April 7, 2014, spectator.org/articles/58651/lois-wallace-rip.

96   *Let go from his company via email:* I discussed the ethics of firing people this way with Jake Tapper on CNN's *Erin Burnett OutFront,* December 9, 2013, edition.cnn.com/TRANSCRIPTS/1312/09/ebo.01.html.

96   *Up in the Air:* Directed by Jason Reitman, cowritten by Jason Reitman and Sheldon Turner, based on the novel by Walter Kirn (Paramount Pictures, 2009).

101 *"The problem with Enron":* Interview with Bill Treasurer, February 14, 2014.

101 *Simone Stewart:* Interview with Simone Stewart, April 28, 2014.

102 *The company's once-dominant presence in Afghanistan:* Richard H. P. Sia, "Pentagon Claims $757 Million Overbilling by Contractor in Afghanistan," Center for Public Integrity, April 24, 2013, updated May 19, 2014, www.publicintegrity.org/2013/04/24/12553/pentagon-claims-757 -million-overbilling-contractor-afghanistan.

103 *"Never rat on your friends":* GoodFellas, written by Nicholas Pileggi and Martin Scorsese (Warner Bros., 1990), based on Nicholas, Pileggi, *Wiseguy* (New York: Simon & Schuster, 1985).

103 *"Someone should have staged an intervention":* Bob Ruggiero, "Could Elvis Have Been Saved from Himself? One Man Says Yes," *Houston Press,* August 1, 2013, blogs.houstonpress.com/rocks/2013/08/could _elvis_have_been_saved_fr.php, 2.

Chapter Five: Fairness

113 *"Be a fixer, not a destroyer":* Interview with David Dawit Searles, May 12, 2014.

117 *Is it legal?:* B. David Joffe, personal communication, June 22, 2014.

120 *"You want your people":* Interview with Ken Meyer, February 11, 2014.

121 *Sometimes favoritism "isn't capricious":* Barbara Moses, "Does Your Boss Play Favourites?" *Globe and Mail* (Toronto), September 10, 2012, www.theglobeandmail.com/report-on-business/careers/career-advice /does-your-boss-play-favourites/article4170253.

122 *Unconscious bias:* Interview with Don Feldmann, April 11, 2014.

123 *"Journalism isn't objective":* Interview with Kirk LaPointe, April 10, 2014.

123 *He makes two columns in his notes:* Thanks to Alan Tecktiel for mentioning this technique to me.

124 *See also the first film version of Levin's novel: The Stepford Wives:* Directed by Bryan Forbes, written by William Goldman (Columbia Pictures, 1975).

124 *"Everyone's a Little Bit Racist": Avenue Q,* music and lyrics by Robert Lopez and Jeff Marx, book by Jeff Whitty. First performed at the Vineyard Theatre in New York City in March 2003.

126 *A hiring decision based on self-interest may not be fair:* Sometimes a family member is a boon, not a liability, to a business. Laura Udall had an idea for lightweight wheeled school bags for children, and when she couldn't find the right designer to create a prototype, she asked her husband, Nick, a professional designer, to give it a shot. Laura founded a company she called Züca to sell the bags, and the business took off. Laura is CEO and her husband is VP of design and manufacturing of the $2 million company. See Geraldine Fabrikant, "Would You Hire Your Husband?" *New York Times,* June 29, 2008, www.nytimes.com/2008/06/29/business/29hubby.html.

Chapter Six: Gratitude

133 *The Berenstain Bears:* Stan and Jan Berenstain, *The Berenstain Bears Get the Gimmies!* (New York: Random House, 1988).

134 *No one is an island:* John Donne, "Devotions upon Emergent Occasions: Meditation XVII," *The Works of John Donne,* vol. 3, ed. Henry Alford (London: John W. Parker, 1839), 574–55.

135 *The psychological and physiological benefits of practicing gratitude:* Robert A. Emmons, *Thanks! How Practicing Gratitude Can Make You Happier* (New York: Houghton Mifflin, 2008), 173–74, citing research by Kenneth Kendler and colleagues at the Virginia Commonwealth University School of Medicine.

135 *"Grateful people report higher levels of positive emotions":* Emmons Lab website, "Measuring Gratitude: The Gratitude Questionnaire (GQ-6) Document, " emmons.faculty.ucdavis.edu/measuring-gratitude, accessed December 28, 2014.

136 *Grateful managers may promote productivity:* Margaret H. Greenberg and Dana Arakawa, "Optimistic Managers and Their Influence on Productivity and Employee Engagement in a Technology Organization," *International Coaching Psychology Review* 2, no. 1 (March 2007), available at University of Pennsylvania Scholarly Commons, repository.upenn.edu/cgi/viewcontent.cgi?article=1003&context=mapp_capstone.

137   *People who kept gratitude lists:* Maria Tabaka, "Increasing Productivity with Gratitude," *Inc.*, September 22, 2009, www.inc.com/marla-tabaka /2009/09/increasing_productivity_with_g.html.

138   *Over half of them were looking for new jobs:* American Psychological Association and Harris Interactive, "Workplace Survey," March 2012, www.apa.org/news/press/releases/phwa/workplace-survey.pdf, cited in Christine M. Riordan, "Foster a Culture of Gratitude," *Harvard Business Review, HR Blog Review,* April 23, 2013, blogs.hbr.org/cs/2013/04 /foster_a_culture_of_gratitude.html.

138   *"That's what the money is for!":* "The Suitcase," *Mad Men*, season 4, episode 7, aired September 5, 2010. Written by Matthew Weiner, starring Jon Hamm as Don Draper and Elizabeth Moss as Peggy Olson.

139   *"Men were less likely to feel and express gratitude":* Todd B. Kashdan, Anjali Mishra, William E. Breen, and Jeffrey J. Froh, "Gender Differences in Gratitude: Examining Appraisals, Narratives, the Willingness to Express Emotions, and Changes in Psychological Needs," *Journal of Personality* 77, no. 3 (June 2009): 691–730, people.hofstra.edu/jeffrey _j_froh/website%20spring%2009/gratitude_genderdiff_JP.pdf.

140   *Both cultures value gratitude:* Blaire Morgan, Liz Gulliford, and Kristján Kristjánsson, "Gratitude in the UK: A New Prototype Analysis and a Cross-Cultural Comparison," *Journal of Positive Psychology* 9, no. 4 (2014): 281–94, doi: 10.1080/17439760.2014.898321.

141   *Cultural differences regarding gratitude:* World at Work, "Trends in Employee Recognition 2013," www.worldatwork.org/waw/adimLink ?id=72689.

141   *Joel Manby:* Joel Manby, quoted in "The ROI of Ethical Leadership in Business," panel discussion, Mike Cottrell College of Business, University of North Georgia, September 18, 2014. Available online at www .youtube.com/watch?v=AwRCcrbEW-o. The seven ethical standards may be found in Joel Manby, *Love Works: Seven Timeless Principles for Effective Leaders* (Grand Rapids, MI: Zondervan, 2012).

143   *Gratitude should flow both ways:* Other books that encourage leaders to express gratitude regularly include Judith W. Umlas, *Grateful Leadership: Using the Power of Acknowledgment to Engage All Your People and Achieve Superior Results* (New York: McGraw-Hill, 2012), and Gary D. Chapman and Paul E. White, *The Five Languages of Appreciation in the Workplace: Empowering Organizations by Encouraging People* (Chicago: Northfield, 2012).

147   *"When an employee is weak in the gratitude department":* Interview with Kevin Kennemer, July 18, 2013.

Chapter Seven: Humility

150 *"I just had the idea for it"*: Interview with Janice Piacente, February 5, 2014.

150 *"The focus is on 'we,' not 'me'"*: Interview with Janice Piacente, January 2, 2015.

150 *"I once had a boss"*: Ibid.

151 *"Humility is not a virtue"*: Hipster INTJ, "Humility Is Not a Virtue," hipsterintj.tumblr.com/post/42156172331/humility-a-modest-or-low -view-of-ones-own. The name of the blog refers to a category used in the Myers-Briggs personality test.

152 *"It's not easy at first glance"*: David J. Bobb, *Humility: An Unlikely Biography of America's Greatest Virtue* (Nashville, TN: Nelson Books, 2013), 5. I humbly submit that humility is a great virtue not just in America but everywhere else, too.

153 *"You can't have one without the other"*: "Love and Marriage," lyrics by Sammy Cahn, music by Jimmy Van Heusen, published by Barton Music Corporation (ASCAP), 1955.

155 *"A man's got to know his limitations"*: *Magnum Force*, written by John Milius and Michael Cimino, based on characters created by Harry Julian Fink and R. M. Fink, directed by Ted Post (Warner Bros., 1973).

155 *Ana Cristina Reymundo:* Interview with Ana Cristina Reymundo, March 24, 2014.

157 *Web of connections:* The phrase comes from Sally Helgesen's *The Female Advantage: Women's Ways of Leadership* (New York: Doubleday, 1995).

159 *Roger Chiang:* Interview with Roger Chiang, February 28, 2014.

160 *"When a writer becomes defensive"*: This is a verbatim quotation from McKee, whose seminars I've had the privilege of attending three times, beginning in the mid-nineties.

160 *"First thought, best thought"*: Caryn Ganz, "Charli XCX: Up All Night with 2014's Breakout Pop Star," *Rolling Stone,* December 12, 2014, www.rollingstone.com/music/features/charli-xcx-up-all-night-with -2014s-breakout-pop-star-20141212; Jon Pareles, "Lou Reed's Complex Spirit Is Invoked at a Reunion of His Inner Circle," *New York Times,* December 17, 2013, www.nytimes.com/2013/12/18/arts/music/lou -reeds-complex-spirit-is-invoked-at-a-reunion-of-his-inner-circle.html.

161 ABC's *Shark Tank* (viewed on CNBC) and HLN's *Dr. Drew on Call* aired December 16, 2014. NY1's *Inside City Hall* aired December 15, 2014.

163 *Warren Buffett:* See, for example, "The Giving Pledge: A New Club for Billionaires," reported by Charlie Rose, produced by Denise Schrier

Cetta, *60 Minutes*, CBS, November 17, 2013, www.cbsnews.com/news
/the-giving-pledge-a-new-club-for-billionaires.

163   *"Be a Jerk":* Tom McNichol, "Be a Jerk: The Worst Business Lesson
from the Steve Jobs Biography," *TheAtlantic.com,* November 28, 2011,
www.theatlantic.com/business/archive/2011/11/be-a-jerk-the-worst
-business-lesson-from-the-steve-jobs-biography/249136.

164   *"If we want to be happy and profitable":* Jaana Woiceshyn, "Why Humility Is Not a Virtue," *ProfitableandMoral.com* (blog), November 13, 2012,
accessed January 9, 2015, profitableandmoral.com/2012/11/13/why
-humility-is-not-a-virtue.

164   *"True humility":* C. S. Lewis, *Mere Christianity* (New York: HarperOne,
2009).

Chapter Eight: Loyalty

169   *Market Basket:* "Are Companies That Value Employees More Successful?" *CBS News Sunday Morning,* aired August 31, 2014.

170   *"Unheard-of in corporate America":* Katharine Q. Seelye and Michael J. de
la Merced, "Workers Win Supermarket President's Job Back," *New York
Times,* August 27, 2014, www.nytimes.com/2014/08/28/us/market
-basket-settlement.html.

170   *Great Place to Work Institute:* See www.greatplacetowork.com/our
-approach/what-are-the-benefits-great-workplaces.

174   *In the film* Tribute: Written by Bernard Slade, based on his play, directed
by Bob Clark (Twentieth Century Fox, 1980).

174   *Loyalty to an organization:* A tip of the hat to Alan Tecktiel for this point.

175   *Paradigm Capital:* Alexandra Stevenson, "S.E.C. Fines Hedge Fund in
Demotion of Whistle-Blowing Employee," *New York Times,* June 16,
2014, dealbook.nytimes.com/2014/06/16/s-e-c-fines-firm-over-whistle
-blower-retaliation.

176   *Philip Davis:* Interview with Philip Davis, May 6, 2014. See also Monee
Fields-White, "Surviving the 'Black Bernie Madoff,'" *The Root,* March
18, 2010, www.theroot.com/articles/culture/2010/03/phil_davis_and
_the_black_bernie_madoff.1.html.

177   *"Loyalty is dead":* "Is Workplace Loyalty an Outmoded Concept?"
Financial Times, March 8, 2011 www.ft.com/intl/cms/s/0
/85ec5d14–49d7–11e0-acf0–00144feab49a.html.

177   *"Now many companies cannot or will not":* Phyllis Korkki, "The Shifting
Definition of Worker Loyalty," *New York Times,* April 23, 2011,
www.nytimes.com/2011/04/24/jobs/24search.html?_r=0.

178   *And Market Basket isn't the only company:* "100 Best Companies to Work

For," *Fortune,* archive.fortune.com/magazines/fortune/best-companies /2014/list. The method for selecting these companies is described at fortune.com/best-companies.

179 *Staying employed at the same company:* Cameron King, "Employees Who Stay in Companies Longer Than Two Years Get Paid 50% Less," *Forbes.com,* June 22, 2014, www.forbes.com/sites/cameronkeng/2014/06/22 /employees-that-stay-in-companies-longer-than-2-years-get-paid -50-less.

182 *Alan Murray:* Interview with Alan Murray, August 6, 2013.

182 *Satisfied employees tend to be loyal employees:* Two studies suggest a correlation between employee satisfaction and loyalty in the hotel industries in Malaysia and Pakistan: Rahman Bin Abdullah, Noraida Bte Abdul Karim, Mohd Onn Rashidi Bin Abdul Patah, Harnizam Zahari, Gopala Krishnan Sekharan Nair, and Kamaruzaman Jusoff, "The Linkage of Employee Satisfaction and Loyalty in Hotel Industry in Klang Valley, Malaysia," *International Journal of Business and Management* 4, no. 10 (2009), www.ccsenet.org/journal/index.php/ijbm/article/view/3961; Rai Imtiaz Hussain, "The Linkage of Employee Satisfaction and Loyalty in Hotel Industries in Pakistan," *Asian Economic and Financial Review* 2, no. 8 (December 2012): 1098–1105, www.aessweb.com/pdf-files/1098-1105.pdf.

182 *John Mackey:* Martha Teichner, "Are Companies That Value Employees More Successful?" CBS Sunday Morning, www.cbsnews.com/news /are-companies-that-value-employees-more-successful.

183 *Employees at those top companies:* Ibid.

Chapter Nine: Patience

188 *Cara Lemieux:* Interview with Cara Lemieux, April 25, 2014.

189 *Jo had a dream:* Chloe Miller, "JK Rowling on Getting Published," *Urbanette* (online magazine), www.urbanette.com/jk-rowling/, accessed January 9, 2015.

189 *J. K. Rowling:* J. K. Rowling, "The Fringe Benefits of Failure, and the Importance of Imagination," transcript of commencement speech published in *Harvard Magazine,* June 5, 2008, harvardmagazine.com /2008/06/the-fringe-benefits-failure-the-importance-imagination; "Harry Potter Author: I Considered Suicide," CNN Online, March 23, 2008, edition.cnn.com/2008/SHOWBIZ/03/23/rowling.depressed /index.html.

189 *Rowling is the richest author in the world:* "Joanne Rowling," *Sunday Times,* April 27, 2008, accessed January 9, 2015, web.archive.org/

web/20110612080035/http://business.timesonline.co.uk/tol/business/specials/rich_list/article3761853.ece.

189 *Her charitable trust:* The Volant Charitable Trust, www.volanttrust.com, accessed January 9, 2015.

189 *Her 2008 commencement address:* Rowling, "The Fringe Benefits of Failure."

189 *"Persistent leaders don't give up":* Steven N. Kaplan, "Persistence Is Best Predictor of CEO Success," *Bloomberg Businessweek Online,* October 26, 2011, www.bloombergview.com/articles/2011–10–26/persistence-is-best-predictor-of-ceo-success-steven-n-kaplan. See also Steven N. Kaplan, Mark M. Klebanov, and Morten Sorsensen, "Which CEO Characteristics and Abilities Matter?" *Journal of Finance* 67, no. 3 (June 2012): 973–1007.

190 *"None of us knows":* Paulo Coelho, *Brida* (New York: Harper Perennial, 2009).

190 *Jeremy C. Park:* Interview with Jeremy C. Park, January 10, 2015.

191 *Delayed gratification:* Walter Mischel, Ebbe B. Ebbesen, and Antonette Raskoff Zeiss, "Cognitive and Attentional Mechanisms in Delay of Gratification," *Journal of Personality and Social Psychology* 21, no. 2 (1972): 204–18, doi:10.1037/h0032198. ISSN 0022–3514.PMID 5010404m. Cited in "Stanford Marshmallow Experiment," Wikipedia, accessed January 5, 2015, En.wikipedia.org/wiki/Stanford_marshmallow_experiment.

191 *A factor other than willpower:* Drake Bennett, "What Does the Marshmallow Test Actually Test?" *Bloomberg Business,* October 17, 2012, www.bloomberg.com/bw/articles/2012–10–17/what-does-the-marshmallow-test-actually-test.

192 *"Life was a train wreck":* Ian Parker, "Mugglemarch," *New Yorker,* October 1, 2012, www.newyorker.com/magazine/2012/10/01/mugglemarch.

192 *Ed Krow:* Interview with Ed Krow, February 5, 2014.

193 *"Brick in the wall":* I asked Ed how he came up with this question. He laughed and replied, "I honestly don't know. Maybe it's a reference to my old days of listening to Pink Floyd."

194 *Employees with difficult personalities:* Mitchell Kusy and Elizabeth Holloway, *Toxic Workplace! Managing Toxic Personalities and Their Systems of Power* (Hoboken, NJ: Jossey-Bass, 2009).

197 *Angry people are at increased risk:* Redford Williams and Virginia Williams, *Anger Kills: Seventeen Strategies for Controlling the Hostility That Can Harm Your Health* (New York: HarperTorch, 1988).

198 *"Short-term myopia":* Robert C. Prozen, "Can We Break the Tyranny of Quarterly Results?" *Harvard Business Review Online,* October 27, 2009,· hbr.org/2009/10/can-we-break-the-tyranny-of-qu.

198 *Companies like IBM and Procter & Gamble:* Michael Schrage, "Are You Driving Too Much Change, Too Fast?" *Harvard Business Review Online,* November 14, 2012, hbr.org/2012/11/are-you-driving-too-much -change.html.

199 *"Effective leaders":* Susan David and Christina Congleton, "Emotional Agility," *Harvard Business Review,* November 2013, hbr.org/2013/11 /emotional-agility.

Chapter Ten: Presence

205 *Ann Zuccardy:* Ann Zuccardy, "How a Brain Injury Made Me Smarter," TEDx Phoenixville, November 5, 2013, www.youtube.com/watch?v =o8HkZgTIYm8.

207 *"More than 9 people are killed":* Centers for Disease Control and Prevention, "Distracted Driving," updated October 10, 2014, www.cdc.gov /motorvehiclesafety/distracted_driving.

208 *Jon Kabat-Zinn:* "Mindfulness," produced by Denise Schrier Cetta, *60 Minutes,* CBS, aired December 14, 2014, www.cbsnews.com/news /mindfulness-anderson-cooper-60-minutes.

208 *"The Power of Presence":* Joe Calloway, "The Power of Presence," lecture from *Presentation Skills for the Professional Speaker,* 6-DVD set (National Speakers Association, 2004).

211 *What can happen when an upper-level manager doesn't listen:* Interview with Silvia Aprosio, July 8, 2014.

215 *"It's very hard for me to process information":* Zuccardy, "How a Brain Injury Made Me Smarter."

217 *Dan Harris:* Dan Harris, *10% Happier: How I Tamed the Voice in My Head, Reduced Stress without Losing My Edge, and Found Self-Help That Actually Works* (New York: It Books, 2014).

218 *Meditation strengthens the prefrontal cortex:* Sara W. Lazar, Catherine E. Kerr, Rachel H. Wasserman, Jeremy R. Gray, Douglas N. Greve, Michael T. Treadway, Metta McGarvey, et al., "Meditation Experience Is Associated with Increased Cortical Thickness," *Neuroreport* 16, no. 17 (November 28, 2005): 1893–97, www.ncbi.nlm.nih.gov/pmc/articles /PMC1361002.

219 *"Workplace Distractions":* Just as Silverman predicted, I didn't finish her article (at least not without interruption). I read it on the *Wall Street Journal*'s website, and to the right of the report was the headline "Bill

Gates's Favorite Business Book" above a picture of the Microsoft maven reading. I clicked on the link and found out that the book Gates was reading was *Business Adventures* by John Brooks. So then I hopped over to Amazon to take a look at it. Then I went back to Silverman's article, where I had to spend a few seconds remembering where I had left off.

220　*Multitasking actually makes us more productive:* Vangelis Souitaris and B. M. Marcello Maestro, "The Case for Multitasking," *Harvard Business Review,* October 2011, hbr.org/2011/10/the-case-for-multitasking.

220　*The entrepreneur David Silverman:* David Silverman, "In Defense of Multitasking," *Harvard Business Review Online,* June 9, 2010, hbr.org /2010/06/in-defense-of-multitasking.html. I learned of the Chinese University of Hong Kong study about multitasking in Roger Kay, "Multitasking: Good or Bad?" *Forbes.com,* July 6, 2012, www.forbes.com /sites/rogerkay/2012/07/06/multitasking-good-or-bad.

220　*Multitasking generally diminishes:* See, for example, "The Myth of Multi-tasking," interview with Clifford Nass, *Talk of the Nation,* NPR, May 10, 2013, www.npr.org/2013/05/10/182861382/the-myth-of-multitasking; Jessica Kleiman, "How Multitasking Hurts Your Brain (and Your Effec-tiveness at Work)," *Forbes.com* (January 15, 2013), www.forbes.com /sites/work-in-progress/2013/01/15/how-multitasking-hurts-your -brain-and-your-effectiveness-at-work; Bob Sullivan and Hugh Thomp-son, "Brain, Interrupted," *New York Times,* May 3, 2013, www.nytimes .com/2013/05/05/opinion/sunday/a-focus-on-distraction.html?_r=o.

220　*People who are truly present:* Katie Manderfield, "Rock 'n' Roll Makeup Artistry: Getting to Know the Walking Dead's Jake Garber," *The Cred-its,* February 7, 2013, thecredits.org/2013/02/rock-n-roll-make-up -artistry-getting-to-know-the-walking-deads-jake-garber.

220　*Ana Veciana-Suarez:* Interview with Ana Veciana-Suarez, July 9, 2014.

221　*Secular Sabbath:* Mark Bittman, "I Need a Virtual Break. No, Really," *New York Times,* March 2, 2008, www.nytimes.com/2008/03/02 /fashion/02sabbath.html.

221　*Our decisionmaking becomes compromised:* John Tierney, "Do You Suffer from Decision Fatigue?" *New York Times,* August 17, 2011, www .nytimes.com/2011/08/21/magazine/do-you-suffer-from-decision -fatigue.html.

222　*"The best decision makers":* Ibid.

225　*A study by the National Safety Council:* See National Safety Council, "National Safety Council Poll: 8 in 10 Drivers Mistakenly Believe Hands-Free Cell Phones Are Safer," April 1, 2014, www.nsc.org/Pages /National-Safety-Council-poll-8-in-10-drivers-mistakenly-believe

-hands-free-cell-phones-are-safer-.aspx; American Automobile Association, "Imperfect Hands-Free Systems Causing Potentially-Unsafe Driver Distractions," *NewsRoom*, October 7, 2104, newsroom.aaa.com/2014/10/imperfect-hands-free-systems-causing-potentially-unsafe-driver-distractions; Virginia Tech Transportation Institute, "New VTTI Study Results Continue to Highlight the Dangers of Distracted Driving," May 2013, vtti.vt.edu/featured/052913-cellphone.html. See also Hands Free Info, "Distracted Driving Studies," handsfreeinfo.com/distracted-driving-research, accessed January 5, 2015.

INDEX